Performing Arts of Chhattisgarh

Performing Arts of Chhattisgarh

Niranjan Mahawar

BANYAN TREE BOOKS PVT. LTD.
7/31, Ansari Road, Daryaganj, New Delhi-110 002

Published by the help of Ministry of Culture, Government of Chhattisgarh

Price : ₹ 500

First edition : 2014

Published by:
Banyan Tree Books Pvt. Ltd
7/31, Ansari Road, Daryaganj
New Delhi-110 002 (India)
www.rajkamalprakashan.com

Printed at:
B.K. Offset
Naveen Shahdara, Delhi-110 032

ISBN : 978-81-905401-8-6

Acknowledgement

We are grateful to

Shri Raman Singh

Chief minister, Chhattisgarh

and

Shri Ajay Chandrakar

Minister, culture, tourism, panchayat, rural development and parliamentary affairs, Chhattisgarh

whose interest and guidance made this publication possible.

To the talented Artistes of Chhattisgarh

Contents

CHAPTER

CHAPTER 1

Performing Arts from Bastar

Muria tribe has got a number of dances almost for every occasion. These dances are called 'Pata' in their language. The occasion on which a particular dance is performed is used as a suffix, for example the dance performed at the Diwali festival is called 'Diwad Pata'. These songs and dances are also called 'Endana'. The Murias call their games by the name 'Karsans'. "The word 'karsana' meaning 'a game' is distinguished from 'endana' 'a dance' rather by its occasion than by its form. Many dances are not called endana because they are not performed either at a marriage a festival or an expedition. They are casual, go as you please affairs for entertainment, and so, though the form is that of a dance, they are called Karsana or games." [1]

The main dances of Murias are 'Diwad pata', 'cherke pata', 'Parli pata', 'Purkolony', 'Mao pata', 'Dol pata', 'Karksar pata', 'Hulki pata', 'Kolang pata', 'Ana pata', 'Ghotul pata', 'Koda pata', 'Dilong or Gedi dance', 'Chherta dance', 'Mandri dance' and 'Lingo pata'. Mao pata is a complete dance drama which has been dealt independently in a separate chapter. Some dances are like jatra or expditions such as 'Diwad pata', 'Chherta' dance and 'Hulki' dance Diwad pata is performed at the Diwali festival. The young unmarried girls who are known as motiaries in the ghotul, assemble in the village ghotul and then sing and dance in front of each and

1. *Muria and their Ghotul,* V. Elwin, p. 556

every house. After this they go on expedition for seven days from village to village in the same 'Pargana'. They cover about four-five villages every day. They perform before the houses of patels, gyatas, gunias and the sarpanchas and sing Diwad pata.

In Diwad pata the girls throw some coins on the ground in the circle of their dance inviting the boys of that village. The boys try to break the circle to get into it. The girls resist their entry. This part of Diwad pata is called 'Mudda pata'. After the dance performance the head of family offers them a basket of rice or paddy and also some money. When the girls bend to lift the basket the boys hit them mildly. The girls through their song requests the cheliks (unmarried boys) not to do so. The girls sing–

We did hit you when you were lifting coins
But it was in love
You don't hit us and
Do not take revenge.

These girls stay in the ghotul of that village where they arrive in the evening time. They spend the night in that Ghotul. The cheliks become their host and make all arrangements and offer them meals of which a few are reproduced here, for example–

The gruel (pej) is made of bits of rice,
Aliyaro Maliyaro!
Where are you going, Alyarsingh Malyarsingh?
We are like a pair of pigeons, Aliyaro Maliyaro!
We are off to search for wives Aliyaro Maliyaro!
What country are you going to, Aliyarsingh Malyarsing?
We are going to Lanjhi Land, Aliyaro Maliyaro!

2

O the sikken horns of the bullock daughter!
I have named a price for this bullock daughter!
Do not decieve me, father.

You are selling me, father.
A rupee is worthless or a broken bit of earthenware,
Yet you love rupees, father.
Liquor is worthless as a horses stale,

Yet you love liquor, father,
And you do not care for me.

3

I have a horned bison, Kopa;
My bison is lost, Kopa
On the hill of sal trees, Gaita,
I had taken it to graze there, Gaita,
I had golden tethering peg, Kopa.
Now the peg stands solitary, Kopa.
The tethering-cord was made of diamonds, Kopa.
Now the cord is lonely, Kopa,
Now the cord is lonely, Kopa.
I will wear the Bharewas anklets;
The anklets tinkle rumjum rumjum.
I will wear the Kochiya's bangles;
The bangles tinkle rumjum rumjum.
I will wear cloth from a merchant's shop;
When I wear that cloth, my waist goes rumjum rumjum.
The neck-band sounds rumjum rumjum.
I will wear a goldsmith's ear-ring,
The ear-ring sounds rumjum rumjum.
I will wear the Kaser's bangles,
The bangles tinkle rumjum rumjum.

Diptong pata or Gendi dance

In the rainy season when the village paths become muddy the young boys prepare gendis. These gendis are made of bamboo sticks attached with footrest again made of bamboo and fixed with longer sticks. Its like walking on the sticks. The length of the sticks is about 6 feet to 8 feet. The first use of the gendi starts on the Hareli Amavasya the 15th dark night of the hindi month of Sravan. It ends on the 15th moonlit night of hindi month Bhadrapada.

The Ghotul of these areas have developed a dance form in which they make several movements making various patterns. By hitting the sticks on the ground they plan their steps. They also collide the sticks that make peculiar sound. Some boys in center of the circle provides music on timkies which are small percussion instruments which they sling from the neck. This ditong dance is a favorite of the Ghotul boys. Gendi dance performance has also been held in several cities and also in Apna Utsava and has been appreciated greatly.

Chirhe Pata

Chirhe pata is a marriage dance of Muria tribe. This dance is performed under the marriage mandapa and this is also known as 'Manda pata'. In this dance there are no restrictions of age. Children, young and adults all can participate in the dance. An wooden musical instrument is made which is called 'Cherahe'. This is fixed on a bamboo stick. On the top are fixed four wooden birds which are attached with strings. When these strings are pulled the birds flutter their wings and make sound. On this sound the dance steps are regulated. The flatter of the sound also make a comic situation. The birds are also symbolic of the bride who will fly away from her parents house after marriage. The female dancers keep small cymbals and make sound which tunes with the sound created by the flutter of the chirahe birds.

The dancers perform around the marriage in slow motion. The songs which are sung on this occasion are called 'Chirhe pata'. These songs are the marriage songs of the Murias. The names of the couple being married, what is the nature of these partners, how do the people around feel about this marriage and what talks are going on amongst the people present there about this marriage are the theme of the songs. Murias have marriage songs for every ritual and they are sung in the ghotul, as well as in the bride's house and under the mandapa. Verrier Elwin has recorded a number of songs.

Kakser Pata or Lingo Pata

Karksar pata is religious dance of the Murias which is performed in honor of their great god Lingo Pen. The Murias tribe considers that they are the creation of Lingo. Ghotul is his greatest gift to them. The first musician was Lingo himself. Lingo had sixteen musical instruments which he gave to the Murias and taught them how to dance. When Lingo appeared on the earth, he was accompanied by the devine motiaries. Lingo created fire and taught its use to the Murias. Lingo discovered mahua liquor. Lingo took the Murias to the jungle gave them the axe and taught them how to cut trees and burn them. For the crops he gave them seeds. Here is a songs in praise of Lingo–

Johar johar O Lingo!
The minda-layre gives out its tune;
Kadur kum it says.
On his waist Lingo wears brass bells;
There are anklets on his feet;
At his lips there is a flute;
From his ears too there burst
Notes of music;
They came from every side.

In another song the Murias say that they sing a song of Lingo Pinnu, Tinnu made the world, made the people, made the kui (Gond tribe), made the pano, made the sahibs, sambhar, barking, deer, cows, roots.

Lingo taught us how to sing
How to beat the tapka (small drum)
How to beat the lisna (big drum)
How to blow the mohari

He taught us how to plant roots and pulses
He taught us to cut forest on the hill side
He taught unmarried boys and girls to sleep in the ghotul
He taught them how to dance and sing
He showed how to do the Meriah sacrifice
He taught us how to cut and burn
For crops he gave us seed.

Lingo pata

O twelve Lingo brothers,
There is haldi and flour for you.
Come Lingo come!
With haldi and flour we anoint you
May songs unknown come to us.
May steps unknown come to us.
The first song is yours, Maria song is ours.
The first steps are yours, Maria steps are ours.
The Maria is the Chelik's
Come Lingo come!

To you liquor must first be given
The haldi must first be put on you
Only with you the song goes well.

Kaksad is beautiful dance which the Murias perform with brass bells hanging on their buttocks its very musical and rhythmic and spectacular.

CHAPTER 2

Saila Dance

Gonds have several dance forms. The most spectacular among them are Karma and Saila. Karma dance is the most popular dance amongst other than Gonds also. Baiga, Binjihia, Kanwar, Binjhwar and Dewar also perform Karma dance. But Saila dance is mainly the dance of Gond tribe.

This dance is performed only by male folk. The dancers do not have any special costumes for the dance. The dancers wear their normal dress while dancing. They put on a plume of peacock feathers in their turban. The dancers hold a small staff, or a wooden gun or an axe in one hand and a handkerchief in another. They also put on iron anklets. The dancers perform in a half round form. One singer starts singing and it is repeated by all others line by line. Saila dancers also go on expedition to other villages. Such dance is called 'Girda' and this dance is as a matter of fact an expedition dance form. The villagers welcome the dancers with honor and they also dance with them. These dancers depart on third day and are given gifts at their departure. According to Shekh Gulab who has worked for very long time with Gonds, this dance was performed in the cantonments of the Gond rulers, which were situated on the hills (Shelas) and therefore this dance was named as 'Shaila' dance. Later on with the downfall of Gond rulers these cantonments were abandoned and the dancers came to the villages.

This dance being the dance of expedition, has become a fine source of making contact and create good will amongst the neighboring villagers. Tribals have such expedition dances in Central India. This seems to be a way of exposure of youth and to choose their partners. The feeling with which these dance parties are welcome and taken care of, shows that these dances have primitive element of choosing their partners. In Bastar also their Chaliks separately go on dance expeditions and they are given warm reception.

Gonds also have a series of marriage dances such as Bhariha, Birha, Kharuva, Sajni etc. Bharoni dance is performed by the female folk. With the dance they sing abusive songs for the family members of the bridegroom. Its a tradition amongst so many Indian communities to sing such abusive songs at the time of marriage and nobody objects or feel bad about it. Hear is a song which is sung in Saila dance–

The village situated on the dadar (platau)
Where blue bull and peacocks are grazing
I will hide you as the clouds hide the moon
The leafs are flying with the wind
I will take you with me as wind takes away the leafs.

I sent a letter through a crow and a massage through a parrot. I am wandering with a dholki and a chikara

Oh! Everyone has a partner but I am alone.
Ar! If you keep patience
Then only you will succeed.

CHAPTER 3

Karma Dance

Karma dance is the most popular dance of the tribes of Central India. It is spread all over Chhattisgarh, Madhya Pradesh, Jharkhand, Orissa and Bihar. Karma means Karm and this is celebration of labour and work. Karmasen is the god of labour which is venerated all over the tribal world of Central India. There are several myths related to Karma. According to one myth Karma and Dharma were two brothers created by Maha Prabhu the great god. Dharma taught the people to live a pious and sacred life. Karma taught them to work hard and earn their livelyhood. Dharmasen went with the Bharhmins and Savarna communities and Karmsen lived with the tribals.

Karma worship is observed amongst the tribals of Madhya Pradesh, Chhattisgarh, Jharkhand and Orissa tribals in the hindi month of Bhadrapada. The tribals bring a branch of Karma tree from the forest and stall it in the centre of the Choupal of the village or at, such place where the rituals and dance is to be performed.

After the worship and other rituals in honor of Karamsen are observed, the young boys and girls dance around the Karma tree's branch.

Karma dance is a beautiful dance of the tribals specially of the Gonds, Baigas, Kanwars, Binjhwars and Dewars. The dance is of fourteen types which are named according to the steps, body movements, styles and speed. Although the Karma dance has its origin in the rituals but this is a dance for all seasons except raining season. At the time of marriage ceremonies, festivals are any occasion of celebration the dance is performed. The musical instrument used is a mandar drum (precusson instrument). The mandar is made of fine clay and baked. It is made by potters. This is hollow. Both ends are covered with hide of a goat or a bullock. It is long drum which is about 4' to 5 feet in size. With the help of strong strings it is hanged in the neck. The mandar is beaten with hands and its sound is deep and loud. When the young boys and girls desire to dance, the mandar players beat the drum and hearing the sound they assemble at the dancing place. Even in winter nights of the hindi months of Magh and Push the dancers perform till late nights. The dancers wear their normal dress. The young boys like to put on turbans.

Karma dance is the most favorite dance of the tribals because it has a lot of variations and variety of folk songs mostly love songs have been developed around the dance. Some of the types of Karma dance are Karma Jhumar, Karma Thada, Karma Lahki, Karma Langara, Karma Ragani etc. The dance which is performed by bending one leg is known as Karma Langda, those which are performed by swaying to and from is called Karma Jhumar, performed like making waves is called Karma Lahaki. In the Karma Thara the singing is done in standing position.

While dancing type boys and girls put on anklets of special type which makes a sound like chhan... chhan... The girls keep their hands on the waists of each other. The boys also stand in front of them in a bending position and singing Karma songs. The girls repeat the lines of these songs. In some dances the boys and girls stand alternatively putting their hands on the waists are holding hands standing in a line. The stand in parallel line facing each other and the drummers standing in between them. Some examples of the dance and songs are given here–

Karma Lahaki–

The creeper of gourd is in the garden
As long as my life has come with its help.

Black dhoti does not have a border
Have you become stranger not recognizing me!
I will be looking at the mango and tamarind trees
For all my life I will be in search of you.

New is the cloth and stitching is on other side on darling when will we able to meet.

The river is flooding and the water might more
Our love will continue even if the police harass us.
On the path (of love) the girls are found
Where ever you live send letters.

Karma Langda

Do not kill the pet bird
The planted tree on sand and the lime without water Dies.
Like wise the lover without love also dies.
O bird! You will fly away to distant countries
And will not remember me.
Cloth can be stitched by the taitor
But keep the love in yours heart.
In the evening time lava bird returns home
You have loved me at such moment.

Karma Ragini

You are plucking the mahul leaves here and there
O beautiful girl! I will not leave you, I will take you with me.
This house is burning in fire and there is smoke in that house
The hearts of both of us are burning, it will take you with me.
This side is flowing a stream and that side a river
How can we reach to the banks ?
We will keep the cooked rice in leaf packet
And water in a gourd and cross over the Dohar hill.
In the plains we will work as labour.
And thus we will become happy.

O beautiful girl! I will take you with me.
Yes! Yes!! O girl I will get your cloth in yellow colour
While going to bathe Jamuna carry a comb
And oil in a golden utensil.
In front goes the nanad (sister of the husband)
And behind follows the bhoujai (brother's wife).
In water they are making fun and enjoying.

In this song the girls are inviting each other to perform karma dance–

O friend! Karma festival has come.
Let us go to dance Karma.
We will worship the goddess Sarswati.
And then Gouri and Ganesh.
O friend! Let us go to dance Karma.
We will worship all the deities of the village.
And salute our teacher.
O friend! Let us go to dance Karma.
The river is flooding, how can we crossover.
Tonight you stay here tomorrow we will take across.
In the day time I will give Khada fish to eat.
And in the night give you fishing net to cover.
But I am worried about my small child.
Who is left at home

CHAPTER 4

Sua Dance and Songs

In the tribes of Central India Lord Shiva is highly venerated. Many tribes consider Shiva as their supreme god. In the tribal myths of creation Shiva has the most significant place. In the myths of creation Shiva and Parvati have been widely mentioned. Goura festival is an important festival of the Gond tribe. In this festival worship of Goura(Parwati) is done by tribal women and the marriage of Shiva and Goura is performed. Clay dolls of Shiva and Parwati are made by the women and decorated with coloured metalic foils of different colours. The festival starts about ten days before Deepavali and the marriage ceremony of Shiva and Parwati takes place on hindi month's Kartika Amavasya(fifteenth dark night) or the Deepavali day. In the nights of this period the female folk assemble where the dolls of Shiva and Parwati are consecrated and sing songs. Drums are beaten and their loud sound spread all around in the village. The songs are in praise of Parwati and are called Gaura geet.

In this period Sua dance(parrot dance) is performed with songs. These songs are called 'Sua geet'. This dance is performed only by women. The dance is full of grace and delicate movements. The songs are addressed to the parrot. Parrot is the symbol of soul and also a messenger. Since ancient times the parrot has been a great of nayikas in Indian literature. The bird has been domesticated by human beings and kept as pat since the early stage of civilization. In Indian literature 'Shuk Sarika Samvad' has been mentioned in several texts. Most of these songs are of pathos.

The women through these songs express the agony and sufferings of womenhood in these songs. Seperation form the husband who has gone to 'Pardes'(distant places) for trade and she is being ill treated by her in-laws, are important themes of these songs. The poetic quality of these songs are very superior.

The sua dance is the most favourite dance of Chhattisgarhi women. They keep a terracotta or wooden sculpture of a parrot in a basket and keep this basket in the centre of the dancing place. The dancers dance in a circle around this basket. The movement of the body and steps resemble with the movement of birds. They move first on the left side giving body weight on the left leg. Then they move on the right side in the same way and move forward taking round of the parrot, clockwise. While dancing they sing suageet.

Most of the dancers are Adivasi women specially Gonds. These dancers perform Sua nautch by going house to house and in front of the house they perform. Every family gives them some money. The money which is raised in this manner is spent on the Goura rituals and festival. The dance is also associated with the paddy harvest and the time coinside with the harvest season. Those tribals who have shifted to the towns to work as labourers have forgotten its connection with the paddy harvest also perform before the houses and shops and raise money to meet out the expenses of Goura festival. Although the dance has a direct relationship with Goura festival, but the songs sung with dance has no connection with Goura worship. The content of the songs is more related to the sufferings of women in general. In a song the women are requesting through the parrot, "Tiriya janam jhan deve", which means do not give us life of women.

In the fourties Shyamrao Hivale and Verrier Elwin have collected Sua songs from the Gonds of the Maikal Hills. They noticed that this dance is performed in the months of November and December which are the months of paddy harvest. But those Gonds who have come to the plains and work as labourers have also brought their songs, dances and other folk lore with them.

Even presently Sua nautch is mostly performed by the tribal women. Goura festival is closely associated with the Gonds, but there is another genre of songs which are known as Goura geet but the content of Sua dance songs have no mention of Goura worship.

The Goura festival is related to Shiva and Parwati and the Gond women make clay idols of Shiva and Parwati and worship them for nine days. On the Diwali day the marriage of Goura and Shiva are performed. There is no rule about the age of dancers. They may be married or unmarried both. Generally from thirteen, fourteen years of age to fourty, fourty five years of age women participate in the dance. About eight to twelve dancers form a group of dancers. Sua natch is performed for about ten to fifteen minutes in front of every house. They are given paddy or rice and some cash by the house lady. After receiving donation the dancers confer blessings upon their family members.

In more tradition bound villages the parrot basket is carried by an unmarried girl on her head and the other women dance around her. The dancers bend forward and move around the parrot in a circle clapping. The dancers divide themselves in two groups. First group sings a line of Sua Nautch then the second group repeats it.

Sua songs have props like 'Tari nari na na', Tari nari na na, more na na nari na, 'Tari nari nara more, nahana ri na na re bhaiya more, 'Tari nari nana more nana, nare bhaiya more tari nari na na', ta more na na suana re , ta more na na, na na suana. Here are some examples of sua songs.

(1)

Go, go, my parrot, to the forest of delight,
to the forest of sandal.
Suana, break off a bunch of mangoes.

How should I walk and how should I fly?
Suana, how should I break them off?

Walk on your feet, fly back with your wings.
Suana, break them off with your beak.

When I return, when I return with the mangoes,
Suana to whom shall I give them?

To the twelve year barren woman, Chandanmati,
Suana, my parrot, you should give them to her.
(Elwin and Hiwale)

(2)

I bow to the moon and sun, O parrot
One shoudn't be born a woman
Life of a woman is like a cow, parrot
Where ever she is wedded she has to go
How so ever clean I keep my husband's home
and break my fingers,
Even then I am scolded by his sister
See how unfortunate am I
The day my husband brought me home
he has to go away to earn his bread.
(Shyam Parmar)

(3)

Moon and Sun, I fall at your feet
Give me not the birth of a girl again
From birth we wretched women are orphans
Mother-in-law, sister-in-law
Are always abusing us
By their continual nagging we are burnt
So I ran away to the forest.
(V. Elwin and S. Hivale)

(4)

The kernel of mango is beautiful the seed of tamrind is beautiful.
Beautiful sister-in-law is bringing water
The Brahamana is asking for alms
If he had come to our house, then we could serve him rice and pulse.
What shall I do of your rice and pulse
What shall I do of your wheat flour
I will go to some other house.

5 CHAPTER

Dadaria

Dadaria is a verse form of couplet, which means a fair of successive rhyming lines of verse. It is like 'doha' of Hindi verse form. Origin of the word is from 'dwi-dariya', as there are two parts in a pulse seed. In Sanskrit literature also 'sloka' is form of couplet. In Urdu literature 'sher' is also a form of couplet. Every dadariya is independent and complete in itself. Dadariya is sung by village folk while working in paddy fields, collecting mahua and other forest produce in the jungle, and at any work place.

Dadaria is sung in question answer style, in conversational style. The content is generally love and romance. When the young boys and girls are working in the paddy fields they make romantic gestures through dadariya songs. They use symbolic language, that is why there is a lot of poetic value in Dadariya songs. When a number of Dadaria couplets are arranged in a sequence and sung with dance, they are called 'Salho'. When paddy transplant goes on, the number of workers required is more and they may be from more than one village or different 'tolas' of the same village. In such case the boy or the girl gives their introduction through Dadariya. They also intimate about the salient features, their clothing, their likes and dislikes and fancies. Through dadariya they also express their love and place where and when to meet. Some times they hint about their villages, their family and their identification features by which the new lovers recognise each other.

Love and Sex are the main contents of dadaria. While working in the fields at the time of paddy transplantation or collecting forest produce in the jungle young boys and girls come in contact. Dadaria is a medium of expressing their feelings. Many dadaria couplets are instant poetic expression. Some dadaria couplets survive for a longer period and become a part of folk lore, rest become extinct. These couplets are generally in question answer style and are addressed to the lovers.

When dadaria couplets are sung in the fields, they are not accompanied with dance. But when a number of dadaria couplets are arranged in a sequence and are sung as 'Salho', can be accompanied with dance. The choice of the couplets is made by the singers themselves. In the dance generally two performers participate. One boy and one girl. Now a days some singers have forward such dance parties and music is also accompanied. The musical instruments which are used are 'dholka', harmonium, cimbals and benjo or casio.

Some examples of dadaria couplets are given here.

(1)

बटकी मा बासी चिमटी धरे नून।
मैं तो गावथों ददरिया तें कान देके सुन ।।

In the tiffin bowl is cooked rice
Pick a pinch of salt
I am singing dadaria
You listen carefully

(2)

You have dadaria then I have karma
In the pallu of your sari my heart is there

(3)

The young girls is going. She is proud of
her youth

डहर रेंगे हलाये डेरी हाथ।
अकेली झन रेंगे बनाले संगी साथ ॥

You are going proudly waving your hand
Don't go alone, have a companion.

(4)

तैं होते पंछी मैं होते छचान।
उड़ाई के ले जातेंव गढ़ लंका मैदान ॥

Had you been a bird, I would be a falcon
I had taken you to the fort of Lanka.

(5)

रस्ता वो रेंगे बाजिन पयरी
हुस्यारी से तो रेंगो ताकिन बयरी ॥

While working your anklets are ringing
Walk cautiously, enemies are watching.

(6)

करे मुखारी करौंदा रुख के।
एक बोली सुनादे अपन मुख के ॥

Brushing your teeth with carinda carissa twig
I wish to listen you talk sweet.

(7)

करु करेला कर डारे चानी रे।
मोर चढ़ती जवानी कर डारे पानी रे ॥

You have cut the bitter gourd in pieces
You have spoiled my bulging youth.

(8)

तोर हो गय आती मोर होगय जाती।
बीच रसदा मा भेंट होगय मिलाले छाती॥

You were coming and I was going
On the way we met, let us embrace each other.

(9)

नवा तरैया मा बैठे हे कोकरा,
रसदा मा रस भागय अनारी छोकरा॥

In the new tank is sitting a heron
On the way the novice lover asks for love.

Gatha Gayaki

There are some ballads in the folk and tribal tradition in Chhattisgarh which are as large as epics. Then there are ballads which are sung by different community singers. The ballad singing is called gatha gayaki. Pandawani, Gondwani, Ramayani are epic level narratives which are sung by Pardhan Gonds and Dewars in very much similar style. The Pardhans sing these narratives and use bana a musical instrument like sarangi. The Dewars use a sarangi which is like a chikara. The narratives contents are common. Dewars call their language of narratives 'Pharsi' by which they mean not 'Khariboli'. It seems Dewars and Pardhans have some connection or common source may be cultural or ethnic.

Dewars have other ballads in their repertoire which are called 'Dewargeet'. Some important ballads are 'pawanras' of warrior heroes. Some ballads are related to their cast heroes. Some ballads are love songs. The ballad of Gopalrai Binjhiya who was the deewan of Raja Kalyansai of Ratanpur is a famous panwara of the community. Dewars claim Gopalrai Binjhiya as their ancestor. Sitaram Nayaka and Lakha Banjara are other famous ballads sung by the Dewar singers. Dasmat Odanin is love ballad sung by

Dewars. This ballad has been spread up to Gujrat by the Dewar nomad singers . The Gujrati version of the ballad is known as 'Jasmaodan' on which a play is written.

The Basdeva community is another community who has s repertoire of Vaishanava Puranic themes and characters such as Saravan kumar, Bharathari, Gopichand are some of the ballads which are sung by these singers.

There are some other love ballads which are spread by the Sufi saints in the medieval period as a message of love. Dhola Marun is one such ballad. Lorika Chanda, Bhujbal, Phoolkunwar, Kanvalarani, Raja Birsing's ballads are sung by Rauts on Bansgeet. Some of these ballads are also sung by Dewars as well. Ballads such as Ahiman, Revarani, Kewalrani, Phulbasan, Phulkunwar are sung by Rauts, Dewars and some others as well.

In Bastar Halbas and Bhatras have ballads related to gods and goddess. These ballads are known as 'Jagargeet'. These ballads are Laxmi jagar, teeja jagar and Bali jagar. The Jagar ballads are performed by the female singers who are called 'Gurumai'. A bow is kept on an earthen pot and its twang creates a tinkling sound. Due to the sound of the twang of the bow these songs are also called 'Dhankul' a word derived from dhanush(bow).

CHAPTER 6

Danda Nautch

Danda nautch is dance form in which only male folk participates. This is very much similar to Dandia ras of Gujrat. The dancers generally put on white or yellow clothes at the time of dance. They use flours to decorate themselves such as garlands, flours as year ornaments, armlets, wrist ornaments and head bands, all are made of flours. This dance is a dance of spring season and to celebrate spring season the young boys perform Danda nautch. The season of danda nautch starts from the eleventh day of the moon light of the Hindi month Kartika and continues till Hindi month's full moon night of Phalgun. In some villages the dance season starts from the Vasant Panchami .In any case this is the dance of spring season although ritualistically it starts from the eleventh of second part of kartika month.

This is a dance of youth. In India the celebration of spring season is described as Vasantotasava in ancient literature and art. The season when the trees and plants and the whole forest is in bloom, makes the total environment youthful. Joy is the expression of the youth in this season. Every young man knows this dance and can perform it with ease. They learn it through their own environment as they see it from their childhood.

The dance is performed in a circle. The dancers form a circle. They have small 'dandas'(staffs or sticks) in their hands. Each dancer holds two wooden staffs or two feet. While dancing they strike these 'dandas' with their own as well as with the other dancers. They create several forms and patterns through series of steps. The striking of staffs create the sound which works as beats through which the steps are controlled. The dance in strait standing position , in bending forward position in moving one step backward and one step forward, taking round and moving forward by changing partners, dancing clockwise and anticlockwise are some of the patterns of dance. The dancers create more than twenty four patterns in danda nautch. This dance has an element of Raslila dance of Braj Pradesh.

Danda nautch is a very rhythemic dance. The rhythem is guided by the sound created by striking the staffs. Sometimes one or two flute players accompany the dancers. They stand in the centre of the circle. The dancers sing some songs while dancing. These songs are called 'dandageet'. Dholak is also used but not always, as the beats are created by striking the staffs.

Here are given some songs for example. Danda dance is started with a prayer song.

First I worship Ganpati Goura
And next Mahadeva
Then I remember my guru(teacher)
In my throat mother Sarswati is graced
She reminds me if I forget any word
If I forget any word (of the song)
I will request my teacher to remind me.

Some songs are based on the story of Rama and some of Krishna.

Without Rama without Sita
Lonely has become Ayodhya
Mother Koshalya is weeping ! Without Rama...
King Dashrath is tossing ! Without Rama...
The subjects are weeping ! Without Rama...
Every one is trying to stop him! Without Rama...
Every one is crying ! Without Rama...
Every body is calling names to Kekai. Without Rama...

Every body is calling her wicked! Without Rama…
Every body is calling her murderer ! Without Rama…
Ram is consoling them all ! Without Rama…
Every one is accompanying Rama ! Without Rama…
Every one is weeping ! Without Rama…
Every city dweller is accompanying Ram ! Without Rama…
Now Ram goes to his mother! Without Rama…
Mother gives her blessings ! Without Rama…
Raja Ramchandra is leaving ! Without Rama…
Every body is weeping in sorrow ! Without Rama…
They have forgotten their own pains ! Without Rama…
Every one has started murmuring Rama ! Without Rama…

Here is another danda song based on the Ramayana episode. Sita has been stolen by Ravana and Ram and Laxman goes in search of Sita.

Ram and Lakhan both brothers going
In search of Sita.
Monkey and bear forces are ready so large that
The land is completely filled with them.
These forces have reached to the sea shore.
With whose power the bridge is made on the sea
With whose blessings they have crossed the sea
With Ramas power the bridge is made.
Monkey and bear forces reached Lanka.
They killed all the demons in Lanka
And brought Sita back to Rama.
Brave Laxman, Sugriva, Angada Sugriva
Led by Hanuman came back from Lanka.
Lanka is destroyed and Ravana is killed
Ram Laxman came home.
Brother Bharat is awaiting them

Everybody became happy
And their arrival is being celebrated in every house.
Raja Ramchandra occupies the throne
The gods are dropping flowers on them from the sky.

CHAPTER 7

Holi Festival and Phag Singing

Holi is the main festival of spring season. In India we have two main harvest seasons, Deepawali of kharif harvest and Holi of rabi harvest. Indian economy is based on agriculture and most of the festival here are based on agriculture related seasons. Spring is also called Rituraj or say king of the seasons. This is time of bloom. All the trees are flowering and the fragrance of their cluster of flowers is spreading in the atmosphere. The plants and trees, animals, insects and human being all are enchanted full of life colour and gayety. According to Hindu mythology the god of creativity Kamdeo is more active in this season. Since ancient times Holi festival is celebrated as Vasantotasava, the festival of spring.

Holi festival is also related to the myth of Prahlad and his aunt Holika. But in the Phag songs this myth does not find any significant place. The Holi songs which are known as 'Phag geet' are mainly devoted to the love of Radha and Krishna. Krishna is in the centre of Indian 'Lalit'(fine arts) and the common folk feels close to Krishnas humanly character described in literature specially by Geetgoving of Jaideo, Surdas and poets of Ashtachap school. The love of Radha and Krishna is the great source of inspiration for the poets.

In the oral tradition the folk lore related to Holi is full of Radha and Krishna love songs. Holi songs are sung from the day of Vasant panchmi. On this day a branch of castor tree is installed on some square of the village where traditionally holi is to be put to fire. From this day the 'Phag' songs are sung. In the evening and night the villagers at some place may be house or veranda of someone or in the courtyard of a temple assemble and phag is sung. The singers and the audience apply 'gulal'(a coloured powder) on everybodies foreheads and faces. The main musical instruments are Nagada, 'dholak', 'dhap' (percussion instruments) and cymbals. Some times harmonium is also used, but the main instruments are 'dholak' , 'nagada' and 'dhap'. The youth express their feeling of love through these songs related to Radha and Krishna.

The Phag singing starts by evocing Radha and Krishna–

(1)

Let us first venerate Ganpati
Whose mother is Parwati
Yes! Gajanan is the greatest of all gods
So let us worship him with full devotion.

(2)

Ten pairs of naggadas(nakkara) are being beaten
Yes Radha Krishna are playing holi
Both are having pichakari in hands
They are pouring colour and gulal on everyone.

(3)

Radha Krishna are playing holi
And have drowned every one in colour
Milk and curd could not be saved
Colour also have to be mixed in them.
Let us all friends caught Krishnalal
And drowned him in the same coloured water.
Then Radha said smiling
Will you like to play holy more.

(4)

Krishna is playing holi in Birij
Playing holi in Birij…!
In whose hands is the big bowl of colour
In whose hands is pitchkari
In Radha's hand is bowl of colour
In Krishna's hand is pichkari

(5)

Come on ! Allaha is playing holi in the war
Lord Brahma has mentioned his marriage in his fale.
Allah is playing holi…
In which month is Allah's engagement
And in which month would be his marriage.
In the month of 'magh' his engagement
And in Phagun would be his marriage.

Some songs are also there which are related to Rama and Sita, in the same style as of Radha and Krishna songs.

(6)

Raghuvira is playing holi on the bank of Saryu
Raghuvira lal is playing holi.
In whose hand is golden 'pichkari'
In whose hand is 'gulal' and 'abir'
In Rama's hand is golden pichkari
In Sita's hand is gulal and abir.

(7)

Phagun Maharaj! Phagun Maharaj !!
You are going, when will you come again
In which month is 'hareli'
And in which month is 'tija' festival

In which month is 'navami' and Dashahra festival
And in which month is diwali.
Which month is Phagun...
When will you come again
In Sawan month is hareli
In bhado month is 'tija' festival
In kunwar month is navami and Dashahara
In kartik is the festival of lamps.
In Phagun month you come Phagun Maharaj
You are going, when will you come again.

In Kadlivan a beetle is humming...
Where was Sita Janukia born. In Kedalivan...
Where was Rama born. In Kedalivan...
Sita was born in Raja Janak's house.
In Avadhpuri Rama was born. In Kedalivan...

CHAPTER 8

Panthi Dance

Panthi dance means a dance form of a panth or sect. This dance is performed by Satnami sect in the honour of Guru Ghasidas, the Guru and founder of the Satnami Panth. Guru Ghasidas was a great reformist. He pearched that the idol worship is not a source of salvation. One should see inside his ownself and find out the truth or 'Satya'. This philosophy was propounded and propogated by some other saints also before Guru Ghasidas. The Nirgunia shool of phylosophy was against idol worship and many saints were followers of this philsophy. According to this philosophy the god is nirakar(formless) and creating his idols does not make sense.

When Ghasidas had this realization, Chhattisgarh was passing through lawlessness. His preachings attracted a large number of masses and accepted his seven creeds. The panthi dance is in devotion of Guru Ghasidas and the songs sung with the dance are called panthi geet. These songs are also devotional songas. Panthi dance belongs to the gener of 'Sankirtan'. This is performed by male and female both. It is also performed in both sitting and standing position. In sitting position this is only like sankirtan. In panthi dance the message of Satyanam(search of truth) is the main content and Guru Ghasidas is Guru because he has shown this way.

The dance is performed in a circle. There are one or two drummers. The drum is known as 'mandar' which is corrupt form of the word 'mridnagam' The mandar is a large drum made of clay and baked. Its one end is slightly wider than the other. Its hollow and it's ends are covered with goat hide. The sound of the mandar is deep. These mandars and their sound can be compared with the 'Khole' mridangams of Assamese and Manipuri Vaishanava Sankirtanias.

The mandar players stand in the centre of the circle and other dancers surround him. If the mandar players takes round clockwise the dancers move anti clockwise and if the mandar player moves anti clockwise the dancer move clockwise. With the beat of the mandar the steps are controlled. The dancers clap according to the beats. The dancers put on jingle anklets. The dance begins in slow motion and gradually becomes faster and faster. The dancers create several compositions through their dance. The creation of tree motif which is now a days called pyramid, creates a beautiful spectacal. Three or four stages are created by standing on the shoulders of each stage and on the top stands the mandar player. Now a days many physical exercises and movements have been incorporated in the dance. The Sankirtan rhythem, slow and fast is the essence of the dance. As this is devotional dance and every dancer sings the devotional songs while dancing, no other gestures are possible. Instead of abhinaya 'angikcheshta' is the important element of the dance.

In the villages where Satnami population is in sufficient number, a pole of wood is installed and around the pole a pucca platform is constructed. This pole is known as 'Jaitkhamb' which means the victory of truth. The pole is painted in white colour and a white flag is hurled on it. The white colour is symbolised as peace, nonviolence and harmony. The panthi dancers perform around these wooden poles. Some measurements for this wooden post are prescribed. The flag's bamboo pole's size is also prescribed. This pole is fixed in a ring on the 'Jaitkhamb'.

The songs which are sung have 'nirgunia' phylosophical content. Most of the songs are composed by the Satnami mahants and the dancers. Here are some examples–

The body is made of earth
The physical corpse is made of earth

How many days will this remain
Tell me.
This body is a toy of clay.
The bed covering are made of earth
Four arms(a measurement) four yards of cloth
Will ride on the wooden horse.
Four saints will carry your corpse.

The body is made of the elements of earth. After death it will again mixed with the earth. The four yard cloth for pall will cover the corpse and the wooden 'kathi' will be taken to the cremation ground on the shoulders of four persons.

In another song the 'truth' is in this way–

The earth lies in truth, the sky lies in truth
The moon is in the truth, The sun lies in truth
The world will survive through truth,
So says the Guru
The stream of nector will flow
You will be able to cross the river
This is due to Guru's blessings.

9 CHAPTER

Raut Nautch

Raut is a community of cattle herds in Chhattisgarh. The main occupation of the community is to take the village cattle for grazing. They have a contract for this job on yearly basis and their year is from Deepawali to Deepawali. On Deepawali festival the Rauts go from house to house in the villages and to those house in the town whose cattle they graze for offering their good wishes. The community considers Lord Krishna their ancestor. Deepawali is their main festival. On the next day of Deepawali they worship Gobardhan.

Gobardhan is the worship of Lord Krishna in the form of mountain Gobardhan. According to Hindu mythology Lord Indra is the king of gods and also the rain god. Krishna suggested his community fellows to stop worshiping Indra. This annoyed Indra and he in his wrath caused heavy rains for several days.The whole Braj was under great deluge. Krishna took all the people to the mountain Govardhan and lifted it on his little finger. He advised everybody to take shelter under the mountain. In this way he saved the life of the Braj people. Since then the worship of Indra was replaced by the worship of Krishna. The Raut make a symbolic mountain of cow dung in the form of human being on the next day of Deepawali and worship it. They also observe worship of 'Matar' which means mother(goddess).

Matar or mother goddess worship is performed in the dahiyan of the village. This is the common place where the village cattle assemble before being taken to grass land. An wooden post is stalled in the centre of that ground. The pole is the symbol of Matar and is known as 'Matar khamba'. On the next day of the Matar puja the Rauts start their dance which continues up to Devaprabodhini Ekadashi, or up to eleventh full moon night of the Hindi month of Kartika.

Rauts put on colourful costumes made of printed cloth may be of silk or cotton. With the upper cloth couri shells are stitched in large number. Two belts on which couri shells are stitched are put on in cross shape covering the chest and back. The tufats of peacock are attached on both sides above shoulders. They also wear a turban. On the ankels the tie dancing belts on which a large number of jingling bells are stitched. When come to dance they keep lathis(sticks) in their hands. They sing couplets. The dance come in a group. The members of the group generally belong to the family of the leader. Generally when approach the house of their jajman they first tie a belt on the neck of the cows of that house. The belt is made of peacock feathers is called suhai. This belt is a magical object which protect the cattle from illness and evil spirits. The couri studed costumes of the Rauts are called 'Jogani' and supposed to have magical power which are also worshipped before use. These clothes also ward off the evil spirits and protect from hostile magic.

The Raut dancers engage the Gandua baja a band of musicians. The number of the band's members are from five to seven. One nishan player, one dhapra player, one timki player, one mohri player and one or two male dancers who are in female attire form the band. The Raut dance is a reminiscent of some ancient marshal dance. The dancers also hold some arms like small swords and shields, horns of stags in addition to sticks. They raise these arms while dancing. First the leader of the troupe recite a couple which is repeated by other members and then dance for some time. Again some other member may recite another couplet and repeated by all others. Generally first couplet is recited by the leader and afterwards any member can recite other couplets.

10 CHAPTER

Baiga Tribe and Their Dance Drama

Baiga is a very primitive tribe of Central India. Its habitat is spread from Satpura hills to the Maikal hills. This area falls in two states which are Madhya Pradesh and Chhattisgarh. Presently the Baigas belong to the Baihar Tehsil of Balaghat which is geographically and enthrographically a part of Mandla district. The northern part of Kauwardha and the north-west portion of Pandaria Zamindari belongs to the high forest country of south Mandla and Dindori. The Pendra Zamindari and the Lormi range of Bilaspur belong more properly to Mandla than to Chhattisgarh. The boundary dividing the Baiga of Jabalpur and Niwas is purely artificial. In Rewa it is in the hills overlooking Narbada(which forms the boundary between the state of Mandla) that the Baiga live.

"This whole region is hilly and covered with dense sal jungle. Amongst the Baigas the Bhumia Baiga is the most primitive and characteristic of all, live along the rugged uplands of the Maikal Range which runs from Amarkantaka to the Salc tekri Hills...But no less attractive are the magnificient of the Supgarh and Baihar ranges, the quint rocky hills near Lamta, the milder scenery of Niwas, the uplands of Mandla which the milder scenery of Niwas, the uplands of Mandla which the blossoming of the trees turns in a fairy land, the lonely reaches of Jagmandal."[1] Regarding their settlement in their present habitat R. V. Russell and Hiralal is of the

1. *The Baiga,* V. Elwin, p. 8

opinion, " There appears to be considerable reason for supporting that the Baiga tribe of the Central Provinces are really a branch of the Bhaigas. Though the Baigas are now mainly returned from Mandla and Balaghat, it seems likely that these districts were not their original home, and they emigrated from Chhattisgarh into the Satpura hills on the western borders of the plain. The hill country of Mandla and Maikal range of Balaghat form one of the wildest and inhospitable tracts in the province, and it is unlikely that the Baigas would have made their first settlements here and spread thence into the fertile plain of Chhattisgarh. Migration in the opposite direction would be more natural and possible. But it is fairly certain that the Baiga tribe were among the earliest if not the earliest residents of Chhattisgarh plain and the hills north and east of it. The Bhaina, Bhunjia and Binjhwar tribes who still reside in this country can all be recognised as offshoots of the Baigas."[1]

The first account of the Baiga tribe was made by W. B. Thomson in the settlement report of Seonee District in the year 1868-69. Colonel H.C.E. Ward was the first to do some what anthropological study of the tribe which he published in the Mandla Settlement Report.[2] He wrote about the tribe, "Wild as the forests they live in…they are independent, high spirited, very well behaved, ready to oblige, and for their absence of dress, they live in much better huts and more orderly villages, than their namesakes(near Mandla). A Baiga village in the heart of Mykul range is a sight worth seeing." Captain J. Forsyh in his book. Highlands of Central India wrote about the tribe, "Far superior to the Gonds in every respect they are the still utterly unrelaimed forest Byagas. A few of these have some what modified their original habits, and live, along with the Gonds, in villages lower down the valleys. They have been slightly tainted with Hinduism, shave their elfin locks and call themselves by a name denoting

1. *Castes and Tribes of Central Provinces,* Russel and Hiralal, p. 310
2. Land Revenue Settlement Report of the Mandla District (1870)

caste. But the real Byaga of the hill ranges is still almost in a state of nature."

"The physical features of the Baigas are like the other Kolarian tribes such as Hos, Mundas, Koles and Bhaigas. "They are very black , with an upright, slim, though exceedingly wiry frame and showing less of negretto type of feature than any other of these wild races. Destitute of all clothing but a small strip of cloth, or at most in full dress, with the addition of a coarse cotton sheet worn cross-wise over the chest, with long, tangled, coal-black hair, and furnished with bow and arrow and a keen little axe hitched over the shoulder, the Byga is the very model of hill aborgine. He scorns all tilling but the dhya-clearing on the mountain side, pitching his near habitation of bamboo wicker-work, like an eagel's eyric, on some hill-top or ledge of rock for earth by an unweared pursuit of game."[1]

This description of the Baigas was given in the year 1971 census report.The socio-economic condition of the tribe has not changed much even in the present times. Baiga remains one of the most primitive tribes even today. They still practice shifting cultivation by clearing forest and burning it.The use of plough is a taboo. They consider the earth as their mother and if they will plough it, she will get hurt. From the hills they were brought to the plains, the place called Baigachak, so that they could settled down in plough cultivation but this plan did not succeed. The government has established a seperate project named 'Baiga Development Project'. Verrier Elwing wrote a classic monograph on the tribe– "The Baiga", which covered alot of cultural aspects of Baigas.

The religion of Baiga tribe is animistic but since they are living with Hindus since many centuries, they have been influenced by their religion. They worship their own gods and goddesses but at the same time they also worship some of the Hindu gods and goddesses. Their chief god is Nanga Baiga who was the first ancestor of the tribe and its founder. The tribe has its own pantheon but no

1. *The Highlands of Central India,* J. Forsyth, p. 359

anthropomorphic development of the gods and goddesses have taken place. Idolatery and iconographic development is absent. The myths, folk tales and folk songs are quiet rich. They have forgotten their original language which was of Kolerian stock and now speak a corrupt form of Chattisgarhi. The baigas have a variety of dances. Some of the dances which are more popular are Dashahara dance which starts at dashahara and continues up to Deepawali, Karma dance for all occasions, Jharpat dance in which the boys and girls try to tease each other, Rina dance in which only the girls participate by forming two groups. Bhadoni dance and Parghoni dance are performed at the time of marriage.

Pardhoni dance drama

In Jharpat dance the boys and girls tease each other. They sing couplets in which hint of sex is made. In the dance the body movements and gestures also are symbolic expression of sex. Bhadoni dance is performed at the time of marriage by the women of the bride side. In this dance the ladies sing abusive songs which are sometimes vulgar also.

Pardhoni dance is also performed at the time of marriage. In this dance when the marriage party comes to the house of the bride the drama is enacted. Two cots are joined in crisscross section and two persons lift them. It is covered with a black cloth and an elephant is thus created. A cloth is made like a rope which is used as the trunk of the elephant. The father of the bridegroom sits on the elephant. He makes all such gestures as if he is a victor. His funny actions and gestures are to amuse the marriage party and to mock at the bride's side. This is an exibition of 'marriage by capture's' enactment. Even today this type of marriages are common in Baiga and Gond tribes of this area.

When the samdhi(father of the bridegroom) rides on the elephant some boys hold the trunk of the elephant and pull it in different directions. The elephant also moves accordingly as if it is dancing. Some drummers also accompany the marriage party. They beat the nangara and timki drums and loud music is created. Samdhi the elephant rider who keeps a battle axe in his hand waves it like a warrior. The drum music becomes louder and louder as the marriage party arrives near the brides house. The members of the marriage party also act like warriors and present different types of gestures pretending as if they are in some fight. They outcry joyfully. They also perform dance all around the elephant making various gestures. All their mime and mimicry is to create an atmosphere of amusement. This goes for sometime.

After this mimcry the marriage party is given proper reseption by the brides side. The father of the bride comes forward and receives the samdhi. He too is ascended on the elephant and both samdhis(in laws) make so many gestures. The members of the marriage party hold the trunk of the elephant and take the elephant here and there. The drummers beat their drums to create loud sound as if war drums are being beaten. Elephant then is taken in side the house of the brides house and in the court yard the elephant dance is performed. Some persons hold the trunk of the elephant and pretend as if they are making the elephant to dance.

The ascendancy of the brides father is symbolic of this capture made by the bridegroom's father in a struggle. The custom of marriage by force is prevalent in some tribes including the Baiga tribe. This dance drama is a remininscent of that custom.

The ladies of the bride side sing marriage songs in reseption of the marriage party. Both the samdhis embrace each other. The women sing 'Dadaria' and 'Karma' songs which have a lot of sex symbolism. With these songs Karma dance is also performed in which the body movements also are full of sex gestures. Karma dance is of fourteen types. These types are named according to the body movements, steps and gestures. Some of the Karma songs recorded by V. Elwin of this occasion are quoted here–

(1)

It was dark in the jungle when my love's
Barat came.
The tiger was roaring Ao Ao; The bear was
Growling Kao Kao.
But I thought of only one thing,
How could I go to my beloved.

(2)

The well is shaded by the trees.
Dont go alone for water, wait for me.
Where is your pitcher?
Where is your gundhri?
Golden is my pitcher
Silver is my gundhri
Dont go alone for water, wait for me.

The marriage party along with the elephant then enters into the bride's house. There in the courtyard of the house they dance vigorously for some time. In the end the father of the girl offers them drinks and meals. The elephant is dismentled and thus the drama ends.

11 CHAPTER

Kamar and Their Dance Drama

Kamar is one of the most primitive tribes in India. Their habitat is situated in the mineral and forest rich hills of Chhattisgarh. The Kamar region falls in the districts of Raipur, Mahasamund and Dhamtari. The habitat of Kamar tribe is situated on the eastern part of Chhattisgarh bordering Orissa. They are still in hunting gathering and partly on agriculture stage. They are good hunters and are expert in bamboo working. They make many types of baskets and traps. The tribe belongs of the Astric group. They had a language of their own which belonged to Kolerian group but have lost it. Presently they speak a corrupt form of Chhattisgarh. The present population of the tribe is around twenty five thousand.

Very few art forms have developed amongst them, but they have a custom of 'capture by marriage'. Around this custom a dance drama is evolved in which they perform this dance drama and sing Dadaria couplets.

Kamars have a custom of marriage by capture. In such marriages at times some fight may take place between the parties of the bridegroom side and the bride side. In olden days it was more prevalent than the present times. But the reminiscents of those fights survives in the dance drama performed at the time of their marriages.

When the marriage party comes to the brides house, the members of the party dance vigourously. They have their arms, battle axes, choppers, sticks and hatchets. They make loud sounds and whistles as if they are challenging the bride's side. In between they sing Dadaria couplets. These couplets are in corrupt Chhattisgarhi language which are romantic in content. These dadaria songs are full of sex symbolism.

After each couplet they dance taking rounds in a circle shouting and whistling loudly. They raise their arms, make gestures as if calling the bride's side for the fight. The marriage party is led by either the bridegroom's father or some close relative who looks strong like a commander. He too holds a bow and arrows in his hand.

After this vigourous dance when the party arrives at the bride's house the bride's father receives the party. He welcomes the samdhi(bridegroom's father) and other elderly persons with his relatives. The women of the bride's side sing and dance. Their dance resembles with karma dance while singing marriage songs. These songs are full of abuses for the females of the bridegroom's family. Those addressed in their abusive songs are the mother and aunts of the bridegroom, his married sisters fufis(samdhi's sister) and other close relatives.

At the end of this dance drama drinks of mahua liquor are offered to the bridegrooms party. The ladies of the family continue singing. After drinks the bridegroom's party is served with meals and there ends the episode.

12 CHAPTER

Chandeni

Chandeni is Chattisgarhi form of the epic (lok mahakavya) Lorik-Chanda. The epic Lorik Chanda although it has its origin in Uttar Pradesh but its found in ballad form in some other parts of North and Central Indian languages. In Chhattisgarh Raut community considers this ballad as their communities great epic. In Uttar Pradesh also the epic is considered related to the Ahir community. Ahir which is a community of cow herdsmen has spread this epic with their migration to different places in North and Central India. Rauts of Chhattisgarh who is also a sub caste of Ahirs sing this ballad on a long flute which is called bans(bamboo). There are two or four bangeet performers. One or two sings the narrative and one or two repeat it on the bans flute. The singers are called 'ragi' and the flute players are called 'bajania'.

The Chandeni ballad is also called 'Chanda Kaini' and 'Chanda Gwalin'. It is also known as Lorik Chanda. The narrative is very large and hence can be kept in the category of an epic. It has been first documented in the Mogul times by Khan khana Abdul Rahim from Uttar Pradesh. Full text of the Chhattisgarhi version has not been recorded so for. The popular portion of Chandeini in which she elopes with Lorik is more popular here. In Chattisgarhi version of Chandeini is the love elopement story of the hero Lorik and heroine Chanda or Chandeini. Both of them belong to the Raut caste of cowherds. Lorik and Chanda both are married to other partners. Chandeini's husband was cursed to remain important for twelve years by the goddess. When Chandeini came to know about this fact, she leaves her husband. She decided to go to her parents house and when she was going on way in the jungle she was followed by Bathua Chamar. She could guess the evil intentions of Bathua and some how escapes. Bathua chases her and terrorizes the inhabitants and try to drive away the cattle of the villagers. Helpless seek help from Lorik to rescue their cattle from Bathua. In a fight he defeats Bathua.

Chanda sees Loriks bravery. At first Lorik was hasitant but ultimately he decides to leave Manjari his wife and elopes with Chanda to Hardigarh. The journey to Hardigarh is full of adventures. Lorik comes to know that all his brothers were killed in a battle and their cattle have run away and they have spread all over Chhattisgarh and his mother and wife are living in a very bad condition. Loric returns to his family but after some time he left every thing and went away. He never returns and not seen afterwords.

Ramadhar Sahu has developed a theatrical ballet basing on this epic. In Chhattisgarhi form of this epic the basic contents are the same as of Uttar Pradesh epic with some variance. The main emphasis is on the elopement part of the epic. In the ballet form there are only two characters, Lorik and Chandainy. All the narrative is in verse and presented by Lorik. He puts on costumes which are normally worn by the Rauts of Chhattisgarh. He also wears a chhatari, a large bamboo cap which is used by the Chhattisgarhi Rauts for the protection from sun and rain. He changes his costumes and does makeup on the stage while singing narrative. This performance is only a small part of the narrative sung on bansgeet.

Rauts perform dance and sing couplets at the time of Deepawali. These couplets have no sequence or any connection with each other. They are also not of much of poetic value. The dance is also just ordinary but the Rauts wear colourful clothes and due to its time, that of Deepawali festival, it adds to the festivity the colour and music. Some of the couplets are given here. The leader of the troupe is addressing his host whose cows he has been grazing.

As you have rewarded me, I will resiprocate.

By blessing to bathe in milk, have children and live for lac of years.

(1)

Get cow wealth and land, get our blessings
Let your horse be filled with grand children
And live a life for lac of years.

(2)

On the river bank is a sandal tree,
And under it is the open yard for cows
Every where white calfs are seen
On the field all over have spread cows.

(3)

The flat land is without grass, there I saw cows.
I saw a man covering black blanket
He is brother of my sister in-law (my husband)

(4)

The pen is shaking the paper rambles
Hence I can not send a letter.
You are not remembring me my heart is tearing
My whole body is full of pain.

(5)

Patrenga bird is beautiful amongst the birds
The nag(cobra) is beautiful amongst the snakes
Kanika rani is the most beautiful amongst the women
The whole world is enchanted of her beauty.

(6)

Washing does not remove the colour of indigo
Iron can not become gold
One may feed any amount of camphor
The crow will not become swan.

13 CHAPTER

Mao Pata of Ghotul Murias

A Dance Drama of a very Primitive Tribe

Bastar is a very interesting district in whole of India with about eighty percent of its population comprising of tribals. This is the biggest district in the country and its area is bigger than the Kerala State. Covered with hills and dense tropical forests the district is thinly populated. There are seven major tribes in Bastar most of them are from larger Gond group. The eastern zone is inhabited by the Bhatras and Dhurwas, the northern zone : on the north and west of Indrawati river is by Murias, the south of Indrawati by Dandami Marias and Dorlas and the extreme west zone is inhabited by Aboojh Marias. The Halbas and Gonds; both Raj Gonds and Dhur Gonds are found through out the district, but with more concentration in the northern parts of Kanker and Bhanupratappur tehsils.

The Murias are also of two types : the Raja Murias and the Ghotul Murias. The Raja Murias are those who have well settled in agriculture and have lost their Ghotul system. They live in the vicinity of Jagdalpur town, the district head quarter of Bastar district. The Ghotul Murias live in the Kondagaon and Narayanpur tehsils which are covered with dense sal forests. Ghotul Muria is the most colourful tribe with their ghotul (dormitary) institution, beautiful dances and melodious songs. These people are very happy people with very healthy attitude towards life. The ghotul Murias decorate their bodies colourfully with the ornaments made of glass beeds and coury shells. They keep long hair and do make up carefully and artistically. The Ghotul Murias both boys and girls are fond of ornaments and put on silver and bronze jewelry. Normally they wear white clothes but while dancing they prefer to put on coloured clothes matching with their silver and coloured glass beed ornaments. Their dancing headgear is made of bore tusks and peacock and king drongo's feathers. A pair of bore tusks are woven with the peacock feathers' fiber in new moon shape and then a bunch of bhringraj birds' (King drongo) long tail feathers are tucked in the middle of the tusks.

The Ghotul Murias have a dance drama form in their artistic performances. This drama is a very early and primitive form which is supposed to have been originated with the cave men. This is most ancient dance drama from where the theatre form has evolved. When the cavemen used to go for hunt to kill some wild animals, they used to perform dances to please the super natural powers to provide them protection from the wild animals.

This was the part of ancient magic with the cave men. After the hunting expedition when they used to return safely with their kill, they used to dance with joy. Through these after hunt dances they used to again show their gratitude to the supernatural who have not only provided them with the games to eat but also have protected from the wild animals' hazards. Up to this stage this was only a dance sequence. The evolution of drama starts from this point. While dancing the leader of the hunters start introducing the element of the story and facts, how they have encountered the wild animal. They describe the whole hunting sequence through mimes, how the wild animal came out of the jungle, how it was gheraoed by beating of drums and bushes from one side, how the wild animal tried to break the cordon and in that attempt it also attack some hunters. Some hunters are wounded and one or two might die also. The other hunters would attack the animal with their bows and arrows and spears. The animal struggles hard to escape, but ultimately killed. All this description is woven in the dance with the help of mimes and action as to narrate the whole story of the hunting in a chronological sequence. This is how the drama originated and evolved gradually with the development of civilization.

Such dance dramas are found in so many tribes throughout the world. In the north Missorry Indians a dance form is found in which they pray their deities to send a group of buffaloes whom they can hunt and eat, such dances also exist in many African tribes. Amongst the Nagas of India, such dance drama is also found. Lumis Havmayor has given a very colourful account of this dance drama in his book "The Drama of Savage People."

In Ghotul Murias of Bastar this dance drama which is based on the theme of a hunting expedition of a bison is called "Mao Pata". 'Mao' in Gondi is for bison and 'Pata' is for dance. This is a complete dance drama which takes about two hours time in it's performance. The time can be enlarged and reduced according to the situation. The older people in Narayanpur and Chhotedongar area informed me that this dance can continue for hours together. At the time of 'Paradh' season this dance is performed vigorously almost every night and for hours till the dancers are completely tired. 'Parad' is a community hunting festival which is observed in the summer season just before the advent of Monsoon. A combing operation of the wild animals is performed so that the animals are hunted for two reasons. Firstly to meet the food requirement of the immediate dry season and secondly to protect the crops from the grazing by the wild animals.

The dance drama starts with the group of young dancers who assemble in the courtyard of the village ghotulgudi. The dancers are in colourful costumes with their drums hanging with their necks. One group is having bows and arrows, spears and axes in hands. The dancers make a circle and dance. In the middle of the circle one person is beating a drum made of hollowed wood which is called Kotorki. Two dancers are having horn blowers in their hands known as tohris. One torhi is made of a bison horn and another of a bronze casted in horn shape. In most of the villages the dancers use large size drums of hollow wood covered with goat skins. But in Garhbengal village the ghotul dancers use the damroo shaped drums which are made of clay and are baked. The earthen drums are made by potters and covered with goat skin by the chamars. These earthen damroo shape drums are about two feet in size and are known as 'Parayee'. These paryee drums are also hanged with neck and are beaten with bamboo sticks. First of all this dance starts with the entrance of male dancers with beating their drums and waving their bows, arrows and axes. They encircle the person who beats the Kotorki. While dancing they form a number of patterns as if to create an effect of cordoning the forest from all sides. These male dancers who are the members of the ghotul are called 'Cheliks'. After a while the female dancers make their entrance in the courtyard. They enter the scene dancing and singing in semi circle shape slightly bending and keeping their hands on the back of the girls next to them. They sing the songs in prayer of their deities to protect the hunters form hazards. After that they wish them to get good hunt and return safely. Some expressions are made in the songs and some are in the gestures. These girls who are the members of the ghotul are known as motiaries. They also wear coloured dresses and silver ornaments which glitter in the moon light while dancing. The motiaries also fix a number of wooden combs in their lobs which are presented to them by their admirers. The more the number of admirers she has the more the combs she has. She exhibits this admiration with pride.

While the dance is going on the motiaries withdraw and cheliks are left on the scene. Then after some time a bison enters in the courtyard. Two dancers form a huge size bison. The dancer in the front puts on a mask of a bison which is made of a blanket of sheepwool made locally. The mask is decorated with cauri shells.

The bison enters the scene with elegance looking around on all sides. Dancing and moving with actions and gestures, the bison is witnessed with cheers by the hunters. The hunters beat the drums more and more loudly and steps of the hunter dancers also become faster. The bison realises the danger and tries to break the cordon to escape. In this effort it attacks one or two hunters and run away. The fellow hunters reach to the spot where the wounded hunter have fallen down. They take them to the sirha the village priest and magician. He comes out and starts dancing before the hut of the Anga Deo. One dancer comes under the influence of the Anga Deo and put the god on his shoulders. He dances with the image of the god on his shoulders under the influence and trance the village priest also starts dancing with all the hunters. He makes peculiar gestures as if performing magical rites. Afterwards one cock is sacrificed and mahuwa liquor is poured on the image of the Anga Deo. Anga Deo is rested on two parallel bars like a palanquin. Anga Deo is in the motif of a cobra hood which is riding this palanquin and considered to be a powerful god in the supernatural world of the tribals.

After this scene the wounded hunters become all right and again they all go in search of the bison, beating their drums. Again they are encountered with the bison. This time the hunters attack the animal with their bows and arrows and axes and kill it. After a successful hunting spree they tie up the game with an wooden post and bring it on their shoulders to the village. They are greeted by the women folk with songs and dance. The hunters also dance to show their gratitude to the Anga Deo and express joy for a successful kill. Again mahua liquor is offered to the god and then distributed amongst all the dancers both male and female as a 'prasada' of the deity. Every one sits in the courtyard and drinks the liquor and relaxes.

In 'Mao Pata' through the mimes the dramatic situations are presented in which the dances produce the actions of the hunters, using their bows and arrows, axes and spears. They also present how they protect themselves from the attack of the aggressive mao (bison). The dancers also produce the majestic animal, how does it appear from the bushes, and when finds itself cordoned, tries to escape breaking the cordon. The attack by the mao, the wounded hunters, the women under grief whose close relatives have been wounded, the village 'sirha'(magician) and his magical efforts, all combined create tremendous impact on the spectators. In this dance drama the Murias not only learn hunting but also learn the rituals, the prayers and the traditions of their tribe. This dance drama is quite a primitive form of dance which must have been evolved before the advent of agrarian system, because in the prayer to Anga Deo there is no element of agrarian society. The dance and drama evolved with the agrarian society must include the prayer to the rain god to give adequate rains to produce good crops.

The whole of the tribal life is woven around their faith in magic, gods and goddesses, ghosts and other super naturals. All these super natural forces have existed in abstract form and they have been afraid of these forces. To please them and avoid their anger the primitive societies have developed a variety of dances amongst them all over the world. That is why the places of dance have been evolved prior to the places of worship in the primitive times. Mao Pata is such a dance drama found in the ghotul Murias of Bastar, who are still in a very primitive state of civilization. 'Mao Pata' thrills the spectator with the beliefs of the primitive mind and the primitive force with which this dance drama is performed.

14 CHAPTER

Bhatara Nat of Bastar

Very few people outside Bastar might be knowing that there is a fully developed traditional folk theatre existing in Bastar tribals. So far nothing has been written about this theatre form, which is known as Bhatra Nat. Even the elite of Jagdalpur, the district head quarter of Bastar district is either totally ignorant about it or know very little. The prominent theatre people in the state neither know, nor care to know any thing about such form. Due to their superiority complex, they look at such forms with contempt. Anything with the tribals is unaesthetic, in their opinion, hence such beautiful art forms go unnoticed from the elite.

In the year 1962 I was at Jagdalpur on the Dashahra day. Late Praweerchandra Bhanjdeo was married in that year and he was to ride on the chariot of Danteshwari Mai as her Chief Priest. Bastar tribals were full of enthusiasm. Dance parties from all over the district had come to celebrate the occasion. Various types of dances were being performed from all the sections of the tribals were there in front of the Chariot. Amongst the dancers I could notice a typical group which was performing some drama while walking in the procession. Some of the artists had painted their faces as some others had put on masks. Some of them had swords and shields in their hands, and some others had carried bows and arrows. I was astonished to aquaint myself with a theatre form in Bastar tribals who are considered quite primitive in the outside world. I could talk to their group leader who was recognised as 'Nat Guru' also. He told me that the form was a 'Bhatra Nat', and was quite a prominent theatre form in the BHATARA tribe. Everybody was so much busy in the celebration that is why I could not digout much from them. My Jagdalpur friends only knew about the existence of Nat form, but nothing more about it.

Since then I have been chasing the Nat and had so many occasions to witness this theatrical form at several places. In the year 1963-64, I had seen the performances in the villages Karanpore, Kumhli, Madpal and Dhanpunji. In the year 1964 I had seen Nat in Bakward village. In the year 1974 I had seen the Nat performance in the villages Jaitgiri, Karpawand and Sargipal. This year I had seen the Nat performances at the villages - Semra and Markel in the third week of May when Nat performances were on the peak. All most every day there was a Nat performance going on in one or the other village in Bhatra heartland of BASTAR district. The area was almost under the Nat fever and charged aesthetically. Every villager was in a festive mood.

The evolution of theatre has not taken place in the Bastar tribals although there are some dances in BASTAR, which has great element of mimes and comic gestures. In Muria Gonds 'Mao Pata' dance, Bhataras' kheluk and Chherchhera mimes are performed to tease the house holders while collecting food grains for a community feast, theatrical element is quite prominent. But a full-fledged feature could not evolve through these dances. But then how has Nat developed in Bhataras of the district? It has got an interesting history.

Some five hundred and fifty years back Maharaja Purshottam Deo, the then ruler of Bastar State went on a pilgrimage to Jagannath Puri with his officials, servants, and a large number of persons from his 'Praja'. The last group included the Gond tribals who were living in the villages around Jagdalpur. The Maharaja of Puri was known as the Gajpati and was also the Chief Priest of the Lord Jagannath. He was the host of Maharaja Purshottam Deo. He was so pleased with the Maharaja that he permitted him to take a sixteen wheel Chariot of Bastar. In those days the means of communication were not so developed to carry such a huge chariot, so it was decided that only icones should be taken from Puri, and the Chariot be made at Jagdalpur.

At Jagannath Puri in the procession of lord Jagannath so many tribal and folk performers were walking-singing and dancing in front of the Chariot, the Kandhs, the Saowaras, Gadbas, Joangs and other folk people from all over Orissa were performing their dances and dramas. When Maharaja Purshottam Deo returned back to Bastar, he also brought some Brahmin families from Puri. As those tribals who had gone to the pilgrimage, they also became Hindus. The Brahmins offered them "Yagyopavit" the sacred thread and declared them as "Bhadra Jan" or gentlemen. These tribals developed a separate identity of their own and known as 'Bhataras'.

The Maharaja of Bastar made three chariots in his state. The roads were not so wide that a sixteen wheel huge chariot can run on them. Two six wheelers and one four wheeler chariot, were made. One Chariot for the Lord Jagannath, one chariot for the State deity Danteshwari Mai and one for the Maharaja as the Chief priest were included in the Bastar tradition. What ever the Maharaja and his fellow beings had seen at Puri have been copied in Bastar district. The Brahmins who had come with them had trained the tribals into dramatic performance. Thus the theatre has been inducted in to Bastar's cultural life. Since then the drama has become an integral part of not only the Dasahara Festival but also of the Bhatra tribe for all occasions.

Nat is an aberavation of Sanskrit word Natya. The trainer is called the Nat Guru who is supposed to be a master in all the departments of theatre. There are very few Nat Gurus in the district and are respected in the society. The Nat is a democratic and secular institution. The whole village is involved in the organisation. When some young and enthusiastic boys of the village express their desire before the elders of the village to organise a Nat troupe, a meeting is called of the elderly and important persons of the village. In that panchayat meeting the issue is discussed. All the aspects of the Nat are discussed. The number of young boys available to participate in the Nat, the amount of money, which is required to meet the training expenses, costumes and other dress material, make up material, musical instruments and petromaxes etc. are discussed. The total initial money is estimated at about rupees six to ten thousand. If the villagers show their willingness to collect that much amount of money, then only a decision in favour of having a Nat in the village is arrived at.

After the paddy harvest the collection of money campaign is started. Some people pay in cash and some in shape of paddy and rice, which is also sold and converted into money. After the initial collection, Nat Guru who is known for his reputation in theatre training is invited to train the young man of the village. He is paid rupees five hundred to Eight hundred for the job. He is the guest of the village and meals, tea, bidi etc. are also provided by the villagers. He starts his rigorous traning schedule which starts in the morning and then in the after-noon after the meals. This training is carried out for three to four weeks. A particular Nat is selected. Generally one group performs only one Nat. The script is known as champu. In Sanskrit the champu means a folk drama and this word seems to have been adopted from Sanskrit. Though the language of the champu is Bhatri but script is generally Oriya. In Orissa also these scripts are known as champus and available in prints. These books are in verse and prose combined.

In Bastar the champus are available in hand written manuscripts and prints from adjoining Orissa. Some Nat Gurus told me that in olden times the champus were written on tadpatra pothis (the palm leaf books) but they are not seen now. One such champu pothi has been collected by Prof. Sarasswat of Raipur Sanskrit College. This champu is on Gangwansh Mahima, or a drama on the Gangawanshi Dynasty of Jagannath Puri.

Initially the Nat has been adopted by Bhataras in the district but gradually other castes who are living with them in the villages have also come in the fold. In Nagarnar village, I met with Limdhar a Nat Guru who is a potter by caste. Nat is common only in Jagdalpur, Bakawand and Bhanpuri sectors, which are situated on the border of Orissa. Nat is also common in the adjoining parts of Orissa in the old Jeopore State, which was also a part of Bastar state upto the early twentieth century. Bhataras are also living in that area. As a matter of fact Bhatras are mostly bilingual and speak Oriya and Bhatri both. In Orissa this theatre form is known as Oriya Nat.

After the completion of the training, the expedition starts to collect costumes and other material. Two three persons, accompanied by the Nat Guru proceed to Jeypore or Jagnnath Puri for purchasing of the dress material, make-up material etc. Under the supervision of the Nat Guru purchases are made, which include papier-mache masks, costumes made of satine and velvet, beed necklaces, ornaments and other things.

The drama is generally based on Puranic themes. The dress material is purchased suiting to the castes of the drama. I have surveyed the following Nats in the Jagdalpur sector-Abhimanyu wadh at Nagarnar village, Jarasandh wadh at Ukunpal village, Kichak wadh at Karanpur village, Hiranya Kasyapa wadh at Bamhni village, Duryodhan wadh at DhanPoonji village, Laxmipuran Nat at Kumhli village. The costumes are very rich and the make up is done in classical Oriya style.

The stage is open on all sides and only the top is covered with a chandoba. On both the sides some wooden posts are erected to tie the chandoba, and to hang, the petromaxes. A passage of about twelve to fifteen feet is left open for the entry of the artists. Rest of the place is covered by the spectators. On the backside of the stage sits the Nat Guru with the musicians. Children sit in the front and then the women. The paddy straw is spread all over the open ground on which the spectators sit. The stage is not very big, generally about twenty by twenty in size or still somewhat smaller. Some thirty years back the oil torches were used to light the stage. Two to four persons used to hold the mashals (torches) and used to move with the artists.

Even today at some stage of the drama when artists at war run to long distances, one person on each side run with them carrying petromaxes. Stage is constructed with wooden planks. The front side is made like a ramp as the artists make their entry speedily. The entrance path is also used as a part of stage. The Nat Guru narrates the text and accordingly the artists act. The action is full of dance and dramatics.

Nagada pair, 'Mridanga', 'Manjira', Harmonium and Mohari (Shahanai) are used as musical instruments. When the warrior character make their entry, they come runnning with their sword or Gada. The nangada drums are beaten on high pitch. The entries of the noble characters are accompanied by the mild music created with the help of mridanga. Jamwant, Hanuman, Bali, Sugreev, and demons use masks, where as others uses only make-up. In one group even Hanuman's face was coloured in deep red and no mask was used. While acting all the characters dance and their steps very much resemble with that of Chhau dancers, Bastar has also connections with Mayurbhanja state in Orissa. The ex-Maharani Pıafulla Kumari Devi of Bastar state was married to the Maharaja of Mayurbhanj Chhau influence might have come with these connections. The Nat starts with 'Purva rang'. Lord Ganesh enters with a mask and stands in the corner. The Nat Guru observes the prayer and requests him to safeguard the performance from the demons and evil spirits. After the prayer the Lord Ganpati gives blessings and leaves the stage. In some nat groups the second entry is made of Sarswati the Goddess of learning with a vina in her hand the similar prayer is repeated and then she also leaves the stage.

Nat and Nati remain on the stage and introduce the subject of Nat. Looking at the audience the nati asks the nat: the sutradhar about the cause of gathering. The sutradhar tells her that they have assembled there to see the drama performance. "Which drama is being staged?" the nati asks - "Kichakwadh" replies the nat. "Oh! that is no good. The honour of women is abused in that, "says the nati. The conversation between the nat and the nati goes on like that and nati rejects one by one all the dramas by giving her logic. In the end the nat proposes a subject on which nati gives her consent and both are happy to arrive at the agreement. After this episode which takes about forty five minutes to one hour, then the nat starts.

The episodes of war between Meghnad and Laxman are 'Meghnad wadh', between 'Bhima and Kichak' is Kichak wadh, Bhima and Duryodhan, Rama and Ravana is Ravana wadh are dealt at length. All sorts of marshal arts such as wrestling, mushtika yudh, gada yudha, sword fighting are exhibited, accompanied by music of 'nagada' the Indian war drums. The spectators are thrilled with the effect of such scenes and await anxiously the killing of the villain king Kichack or demon king Rawana. In the eleventh twelveth century when the Sanskrit drama degenerated and confined itself to the courts of the Indian Rulers, a new theatre with the patronage of the traditional and folk vitality developed in India. This theatre form which was based on Purana themes became so popular in the masses that it had worked as an instrument of ethical and cultural education of the people for a very long time. In the medieval India and Islamic influences spread rapidly under the protection of Moslem rulers at Delhi, the folk theatre counter acted it by creating deep sense of faith towards the Bhagwat Dharma. People identified with the goodness and virtues of Bhagwat Dharma and looked with contempt towards the offenders. Even today the identification of the audience with the noble characters is so intense, that when the Hiranya-Kashyap or Ravana is killed, the spectators endorse it with loud cheers and applause.

The nat is like a festival with the Bhatra people. They abstain from the work to see nat. Announcement of nat performance is made in the near by weekly 'hats' by the Kotwar of the village, where villagers from all the surrounding area come. This announcement is enough, and all the people in that vicinity come to know about it. The villagers construct gates to welcome the spectators. Whole village especially the roads leading to the ground where the nat is to be exhibited are decorated with mango leaf hangings. Tea vendors, pan-bidi shops, fruit vendors and snack vendors also reach there. Generally the number of the spectators is from three thousand to ten thousand. The nat starts at about ten o' clock in the night and continues till morning. Generally there does not arise any law and order situation. All the problems are tackled by the village people though one or two policemen may also be present from near by police station.

Nat is a very powerful and effective theatre in Bhatra area of Bastar. It will continue to be so far a distant future. Why this form has not been adopted by other tribes specially the Murias who are so fond of fun and entertainment is a riddle. Bhataras consider nat as their cultural identity and feel proud of it.

New Experiment in Bharat Nat

Most of the plays of Bhatra Nat are based on the themes of Mahabharata and Ramayana epics therefore this theatre form can be put under the category of traditional theatre. In Bastar the Bhatras are the main participants in this theatre form due to which the theatre form has been named on their caste name. But in the adjoining part of Oriassa, Gond, Bhatra, Panka, Dome and other Hinduised low castes have started to participate in it. The experiments, which are taking place in the western Orissa, are also influencing the Nat in Bastar. There are several castes, which are found commonly in Western Orissa and Bastar as it is contiguous region. The people living together in the same region in the villages and small towns participate jointly in the Nat performances. Although the Nat themes are based on Puranic texts but the character of the Nat reportories are secular and democratic. The Nat guru (the theatre director) can be of any caste and so are also about the other actors.

The old books of Nat champus are mostly hand written and a few old manuscripts on palm leaf are still in existence. Recently several champus have been printed in Oriya scripts and they are available in bookshops. The Bhatras are found in Bastar and Orissa both and they are bilingual. As a matter of fact, Bhatra is a corrupt form or Oriya language and the Bhatras can speak and read Oriya with little effort. The people, who are going to Orissa, bring new champus for their performances. Some local Nat Gurus also prepare new plays on contemporary themes and perform such productions. I have already mentioned about two such plays; 'Indira Gandhi Nat' and 'Adiwasi Nat'. Recently I had an opportunity to see such a new Nat "Jangal Samrat Tarjan Wadh" in Bastar by an Orissan Nat Troupe, which came from Padampur village of Orissa.

I was tempted towards this Nat when came to know the name of the play. I was startled when I heard the name of the play. I have already mentioned that most of the Nat troupes prepare only one play. On my enquiry the Nat Guru told me that their troupe previously used to perform 'Jaydrath Wadh Nat' a play based on the epic Mahabharata. The script was written by the Padampur troupes Nat Guru himself. The theme of the play is summarized here–

Once a prince went to the jungle with his father on hunting expedition. He got separated from his father during the course of hunting. The king sent several servants in search of the prince but he could not be found. One day a Saoura hunter went on hunting. He heard the voice of a child who was weeping. He went towards that side from which direction the voice was coming. He found a very beautiful child who was weeping. He was very much surprised to see that child in the jungle. That Saoura was also childless therefore he thought that the boy was a gift of god to him and he brought with him and adopted the child. He loved the child and brought him with affection. He used to take the boy with him to the jungle for hunting. He brought him up like a Saoura. The boy picked all the habits of Saoura and was grown up amongst the other Saoura boys. His total behaviour was of a Saoura. In due course he forgot that he was a prince and other memories of his early childhood life. He thought himself to be a Saoura.

When the Saoura and his wife became old and weak they called the boy and gave him a bowl and said, "Now we are old and cannot go for hunting, so it is now your duty to go for begging to support us. You should also go to the forest to collect roots and shoots to eat. In those days the king of the neighbourhood state was worried about his daughter's marriage, as he was not getting a proper match for her. His daughter Raskala was young and beautiful. When Narada Muni came to know about the worries of the king, he went to meet him. The king told Narada Muni about his worries. Naradji assured the king, "Dont worry, O Raja, I am always wandering on this earth. I will definitely find out some good match for your daughter. You should not worry now".

Narad Muni straight away went to the house of that Saoura and met the prince. He proposed to the boy to marry the princess Raskala. The boy said, "I am son of a poor Saoura, how can I dream of marrying a princess? Dont you see that I am begging to feed my old parents?" Then Narad Muni told him about his past life and how he was separated from his father while they were on hunting expedition. When the boy came to know that he too is a prince, then he agreed to marry the princess Raskala. Naradji arranged their meeting at a place in the forest.

When the princess was waiting for the prince to come in the forest at that time the Jungle Samrat (emperor of the forest) came there and forcibly kidnapped her. When the prince came to that spot he did not find the princess there. Naradji told him that the emperor of the forest Tarjan has kidnapped hi would be wife and he should chase him and fight with him to get the princess. The prince chasing them went to his palace and challenged the Jungle Samrat Tarjan. There was a great fight between them and in that fight the prince killed Tarajan. The prince took the princess to her father and there they were married ceremoniously. The king, Raskala's father gave his kingdom to the prince.

Now let us analyse the theme of this play. This play has nothing to do with the theme of famous story of Tarjan in which a child was taken away by a chimpanzee and who was brought up amongst the chimpanzees. The name of Tarjan has been used because of the popularity of the movies of this title. Tarjan is a villain in this play. If we replace the name of Tarjan with some Puranic character say for example with Rawana, then the whole play would appear like a traditional play based on Ramayana. There is already such a Nat play: Rawana Wadh. The complete structure and theme of this play is similar to that of the Puranic based theme plays. Only for creating change the name of Tarjan has been adopted in place of any Puranic character.

I had a long discussion with the Nat Guru of Jungle Samrat Tarjan. He told me that spectators are desiring for new themes and new plays. The traditional Nat goer is now able to see cinema and films on television and videos. They are exposed to new sources of entertainment and are being influenced by these new sources. We have also prepared ourselves for the changing circumstances and to meet the demands of the audience. We must try to incorporate new characters, new themes in the Nat plays. We have done this experiment on these lines. Some other Nat Gurus are also trying to write some new plays.

Although minor changes and a few experiments are being attempted in the Nat theatre tradition, but the tradition is so strongly deep rooted that much deviation does not look possible atleast in the near future.

Kichaka Wadh Nat Performance

The episodes which are related with fighting between the characters of the Mahabharata and Ramayana epics are more popular amongst the Nat performers. 'Kichaka Wadh' Nat is one of the most popular episodes of Bhatra Nat. There is a lot of dramatic element in this play continues to be favourite with the audience. I am presenting some excerpts here from 'Kichaka Wadh Nat'. The Kichaka Wadh episode appears in the 'Virat Parva' of Mahabharta.

When the Pandavas were passing their time in the wanvas (living in forest) for twelve years, they were worried about the end of that period because the last thirteenth year they had to spend in hiding. They were thinking, "How and where to spend the thirteenth year so that the Koravas are not able to know about them." They decided to spend their thirteenth year in Viratnagar the capital of Matsya kingdom. "The king of Matsya is our sympathizer also", said Yudhisthir. "He is religious old man, liberal and always friendly towards us," further added Yudhisthir.

Then they planned how to go and join in the services of King Virata. Yudhisthir said, "I am a trained dice player, so I will join his service in that capacity as a Brahmiin whose name would be Kanka." Bhim said, "I will join as a cook and my name will be Ballava." Arjuna said, "I will join as a dancer eunuch my name will be Vrahnala". Sahdeo said, "My name will be Tantipal and I will take care of the cows and other cattle of the king". Nakul said, "I will take care of his horse stable and my name will be Granthika". Dropadi said, "I will serve as a personal maid-servant of the queen and my name will be Sarandhri". This is what the Pandavas decided and went to the king Virata and joined in his service.

Performance

The nat and nati enter on the stage. The nati looks all around and exclaimed to see so many people gathered around. She performs a bit of dance and asks the nat, "Why all these people have come here?"

This is the prekchhaka samaj who have assembled to see the nat performance," said the nat. Nati : "So which Nat should be presented tonight?"

Nat : I think Kumbhakaran Wadh Nat will be nice to perform."

Nati : "No, no! This samaj (audience) has already seen that Nat a few days back."

Nat : "Then Dushashan Wadh Nat will be good".

Nati rejects this proposal also by giving this or that agreement. Then the nat proposes the "Bali Wadh Nat" but it was also rejected by the Nati. Then the nat asks her to suggest some Nat.

Nati, "What do you think of Kichaka Wadh Nat? In my

opinion this will entertain the samaj and at the same time this Nat establishes the victory of the virtue on the evil."

The nat is pleased on the suggestion and accepts it. Both of them dance together and goes in the background. This episode takes about twenty minutes.

Then palace scene is shown. The king and the queen are sitting on the chairs and discussing about the palace problems and the new servants. At the same time Dropadi enters with a bowl containing oil in it. She requested the queen to let her apply oil and comb her hair. The king looks at Dropadi and asked about her, "Who is this girl? I have not seen her in the palace before." The queen replied, "She is my maid servant. She was serving the Pandava queen Dropadi but as the Pandavas have gone to live in jungle, she has come here to serve me." After this the king Virata left the stage and Dropadi applied oil and combed queen's hair. She made a hairbbun and fixed some flowers in it. When Sairandhri was doing all that, Kichaka came to the palace to meet his sister, the queen.

When Kichaka saw a beautiful young woman serving the queen in her palace, he asked about her–

"Who is this woman, O sister! I have not seen her in the palace before. From where have you got her?"

The queen replied–

"She is my new maid servant Sairandhri". Kichaka who was the chief of the army of king Virata and was the brother of the queen was attracted towards the beauty of Sairandhri. He was full of lust and was tempted towards her. He went near to his sister and said,

"O Sudeshna! I am being attracted towards this girl. Her sweet fragrance is tempting me like a fine liquor." Kichaka looks at Sairandhari with lust. Sairandhri is not raising her eyes and continues to look at her feet. Kichaka is continuously looking at her with lust and said–

"O my nice sister, who is this woman? Whose wife is she and where has she come? She is agitating my heart. She is making me ill and unless and until I get her, I will not become alright."

Kichaka again looks at Sairandhri with full of lust and again spoke thus–

"Oh sister! This is not proper for this beauty to serve here as a maidservant. I have never seen such a beautiful woman before. I wish that she should become my wife and rule over my heart and enjoy all my wealth. I have elephants, a number of horses and chariots. I have a big force of servants. There is no dearth of fine drinks and food in my palace. I wish her to be my wife and to live there. She should grace my palace by becoming my queen."

After getting permission from the queen Kichaka went near to Sairandhari and started praising her beauty in several ways–

"You are the most beautiful woman in the world. Your face is beautiful like a full moon. Your eyes are like lotus petals. Your voice is as sweet as cuckoos cooing. You are the true incarnation of goddess Laxmi. Are you really Rati who sports with Kamadeo? Your half-open eyelids are so pleasing as the moonlight. Your breasts are finely shaped... O beautiful woman, if you wish I will leave all my other wives. They will always be in you service. O pretty woman, I will also serve you like your slave."

Looking to his advances Sairandhari rebuked him,

"O Kichaka! Its not good for you to desire me to become your wife. You are a great army chief of this kingdom and I am only an ordinary servant. You have already wives, better love them. You will be happy if you love your wives. You very well know that whatever you are desiring is a sin. It will bring you bad name.

But Kichaka was obsessed by lust. He was insisting her to marry him. Then Sairandhari spoke thus to him,

O Kichaka listen! I am a married woman. You should not desire to get other's wife. It is sin. You will be defamed and dishonoured if you wish to marry me."

Kichaka : "O beautiful woman! You should not refuse me like this. I am your slave, your servant. If you refuse to become my wife then you will have to repent. I am the ruler of this kingdom. There is no one on this earth who can mach me in strength. I am handsome, the most fortunate person who possesses all the comforts and pleasures of life. I will present you this kingdom. Why do you want to remain just a maidservant? You should marry me and enjoy all these comforts."

Kichaka was adamant and insistent. When Sairandhari realised that Kichaka's intentions were sinful then she became angry and spoke thus :

"O you son of a charioteer! Dont desire to get me. Do not risk your life. You should know that five brave and dangerous Gandharavas are my husbands. They are always around me and take care of me. You can never get me. They will kill you. You should forget about me otherwise you would be completely destroyed. O son of a charioteer it seems your end is near." If you try to dishonour me, you will be killed by my five brave Gandharva husbands. None can protect you from their wrath."

Sairandhari rejected the proposal of Kichaka, which annoyed him greatly. One day he went to his sister queen Sudeshana and spoke to her thus:

"O sister, you any how convince Sairandhari to marry me otherwise I will kill myself. If you want to see me alive please, prepare her to be my queen".

She spoke to Kichaka :

"O brother! This Sairandhari has taken my shelter. She is a virtuous woman. No other person with sinful intentions can touch her. I have heard that her five Gandharva husbands are always around to protect her. I cannot convey your message to her. She had told me that if her honour would be hurt, her Gandharva husbands would not spare the person. You are my brother that is why I warn you not to behave like this."

But Kichaka was mad due to lust and sex. so he said, "O sister! Dont tell me about the Gandharvas. What to say of five Gandharvas I am strong enough to kill hundreds of Gandharvas alone!"

Then Sudeshna started crying. She murmured, "Oh! This would be great sin! This would bring great disaster." Presuming of the future calamities she started weeping, and spoke thus :

"O you immoral and sinful Kichaka! Due to you all my brothers and clan members will be killed. Now it seems definite that your end is near. You want to involve me in such an immoral act which is not at all worth doing." Even realizing all the consequences fully well she agrees to help her brother in his sinful act due to her affection towards her brother. She said,

"I know you will destroy your whole clan and relations."

Now Sudeshna is planning how to arrange Sairandhari's meeting with Kichaka. She after thinking spoke to Kichaka, "O Kichaka, you get prepared some delicious food and drinks on some festival day. I will send Sairandhari to your palace to bring some fine drinks. There you both will be alone and you can win her heart in your favour. She may agree to have love with you in that lonliness."

According to the plan one day Kichaka arranged everything and invited Sudeshna on meals. He was very much impatient to get Sairandhari. Sudeshna sent Sairandhari to Kichaka's palace to bring some fine drinks.

"I am very thirsty, go and bring some fine liquor." said Sudeshna.

"O queen! Do not send me to his palace. You know how immoral and shameless he is," said Sairandhari.

Sudehna, " I assure you, he will not do anything against your wishes."

When the queen insisted so much, Sairandhari went to Kichaka's palace with a golden jar to bring fine drinks. She was scared but she was compelled to go there due to the queen's order. Kichaka tried to seduce her. He offered her gold ornaments, precious jewelry and silk clothes. He offered her a nice bed to sit with him and make love. Sairandhari refused to accept anything and said, "The queen has sent to take drinks for her." After that Kichaka caught her arm. Sairandhari cried.

"O raskal! Leave me! It seems you are inviting your death!" Saying this she started running from there. Kichaka caught her upper cloth and started pulling it. Sairandhari pushed him with her full strength and he fell down. Sairandhari immediately ran towards the king's court. Kichaka chased her and caught her by her hair and gave her a kick. Sairandhari fell on the floor in the king's court. Blood was oozing from her mouth. The members of the king's court condemned Kichaka's act but the king was sitting silent. He was old and weak and afraid of Kichaka. Yudhishthira and Bhima were also present there. Bhima was full of anger but Yudhishthira through his gestures instructed him to maintain calmness. Such a behaviour from the king, she did not expect. Then she rebuked him for his inaction and went to the queen's palace. Before leaving the court she addressing the king Virata, spoke thus,

"You being the king are not behaving like a king in the interest of justice. O king you are behaving like a khangar (robber). Before your eyes this Kichaka has kicked me, which cannot be justified. All your council members have witnessed this behaviour. Even then you people are sitting calmly as if nothing has happened. Kichaka is immoral but it seems the king and his council members have also forgotten their religious duty."

When she entered into Sudeshna's palace she was weeping. Sudeshna asked her, "Why are you weeping? Who has beaten you? Who has hurt you? What has happened to you? Tell me." Then Sairandhari said, "You know everything. You had conspired to send me to your brother's palace for bringing drinks. Now you are behaving like an innocent person as if nothing has happened."

Sudeshna tried to pacify Sairandhari in several ways but she was not. Then Sudeshna assuring her said, "If you want, I will get him punished." On hearing this Sairandhari said, You need not punish him. He will be sent to Yamloka by my Gandharva husbands with whom he is committing this crime by abusing their innocent wife."

Dropadi was burning with anger and was thinking what to do. If Kichaka was not killed he would again try to abuse her. Her honour was not safe. She thought in her heart, "Only my husband Bhimsen can help me and do my desired work. Thinking so she went to Bhimsen's place in the night. Bhimsen was also enraged with

Kichaka's behaviour and was restless. He too was not getting sleep. She went there and said,

"How are you sleeping so nicely, when the great sinner who has insulted me is still alive!" She awoke him and embraced him in her arms tightly and started weeping. She said,

"O Bhimsen get up! Your wife is being insulted before your eyes and even then you are sleeping. How can such an immoral person remain alive even after insulting your wife?"

Spoke Bhima, " O Dropadi, why are you so sad? Why are you looking so pale and weak? What do you want me to do for you?"

Dropadi, "You know everything and even then you are asking me, why am I so sorry?" Then she again said,

"The army chief of the king whose name is Kichaka is his brother-in-law. Every day he is coming to me and compelling me to become his wife. My honour is not safe here. This shameless proposal is killing me. You are the strongest amongst the Pandava brothers, therefore I have come to you." I have reached to this position because of your eldest brother who is a gambler and always busy playing dice. After all I am also princess, daughter of king Drupad. Because of your brother I was insulted by the Koravas before everybody. I am living here as a maid servant due to him only."

"The great warrior archer Arjun is living like eunuch here teaching dance. Now think about you, O Bhima! You are the strongest person on this earth and here you are working like Ballava (cook) in the palace of king Virata. I am ashamed to see you Pandava brothers in this condition."

"Younger brother is grazing cows. When I see him in this condition, my heart starts sinking. He has never committed any sin. Only because of his eldest brother he is compelled to work like a cow-heard."

"Your brother Nakul who is full of wisdom and is a great warrior is serving in the king's stable looking after his horses. Your brother Yudhishthir is responsible for all these sorry conditions."

"Due to your gambler brother I am working as a maid servant in this palace arranging for bathing articles. I am making arrangements for her toilet."

Bhimsen was moved by Dropadi's words. His eyes were full of tears. He spoke thus with heavy heart to her, "O Dropadi, I understand your condition. I would have killed Kichaka in the king's presence only but because of my elder brother's instructions I did not do anything. We are in hiding and a few days are left when our hiding period will be completed. I swear you, then I will kill this Kichaka and avenge the insult he has committed on you."

Dropadi hearing the words of Bhima said, "I am not going to wait for so many days. I am afraid he will again try to dishonour me. He is a favourite of the king, therefore he is not afraid of anybody. Bhima, if you cannot kill him before sunrise, then I will take poison and finish myself." After saying so, she put her head on his chest and started weeping.

Then Bhima assured her saying. "O Dropadi! Do not be mad. I swear you that I will kill him and all his brothers before sunrise. You approach him and invite him to meet you in the dancing hall of the palace. I will be waiting for him there."

Next morning Kichaka went to Sairandhari and spoke to her, "Sairandhari, yesterday I kicked you before the king and nobody could save you. Here I am all in all and the king or anyone else cannot dare to protect you. It will be wise on your part to accept me as your husband and enjoy all the luxuries and the wealth in my possession. I will provide you hundreds of servants."

Then Sairandhari spoke thus, "O Kichaka, if you really love me then come to meet me in loneliness. Nobody should know about our meeting because I am afraid of the anger of my Gandharva husbands. If you assure me to do this then I can come to meet you."

When Kichaka assured her of this she said, "Kichaka, you come to meet me in the night in the dancing hall of the palace. This is a lonely, safe place," so hearing Kichaka departed happily.

Sairandhari went to the kitchen and informed Bhima about the scheme. He was pleased to know that. Dropadi said, "O Bhima! Tonight Kichaka is coming alone to the dancing hall. Now you must kill that rascal and do not miss this opportunity." saying this Dropadi departed.

Bhimsen went to the dancing hall in the night. The dancing hall was completely dark. Bhima lied down on the bed covering him with a female sari. Kichaka came there and sat on the bed by the side of Bhima and touched him thinking that Sairandhari was waiting for him. He was making self-praise about himself that even his wives tell him that there is none more handsome person in the world than him. He boasted, "I have immense wealth, elephants, horses and hundreds of servants. Today I present you everything, which is mine. I have many luxurious things to enjoy. Now all those things I offer you."

Hearing all this, Bhima said, "You must be feeling my delicate touch. You are very clever in this art. There is none who is better than you in the art of seducing women." Saying this Bhima jumped from the bed and caught hold of his hand and said, "Although you are as big as a mountain, but today I will drag you on the floor like a lion drags an elephant." After that Bhimsen caught hold of his hair. Kichaka freed himself with a jerk and caught Bhima. Then both started fighting. They were attacking each other. They were challenging each other and roaring like tigers. First they were wrestling. This episode continued for about fifteen minutes. Afterwards they fought with their clubs (gada-yudha). This episode also continued for about twenty minutes and then they threw their clubs aside. After they came to boxing (mushti yudha). In this episode they also tried wrestling tricks on each other. Ultimately Bhima gave him a powerful blow and Kichaka fell on the floor. Bhima caught his hair and lifted him on his both hands and threw him on the stage and sat on his chest and gave him a powerful blow on his chest. Kichaka died with his blow. Bhima dragged the body of Kichaka on all the corners of the stage. This episode continued for about forty-five minutes.

The spectators of Bhatra Nat enjoy such episodes in which fighting scenes are presented. Now a days the actors have started copying the filmy style fighting in the Nat. They also wear canvas shoes to make the fighting scenes interesting. The Nat ends in the early morning with some dance and song.

CHAPTER 15

Nautcha

A Folk Theatre of Peasantry from Chhattisgarh

In central India we find a number of folk theatre forms in existence. The evolution of theatre had taken place in the most aboriginal tribes of this area. The Maria Gonds of Bastar have a majestic dance; the bison horn dance, which is performed with a headgear made of bison horns. This dance has combined dramatic gestures in it with great skill. The ghotul Murias have a fully developed dance drama form known as 'Mao Pata'. Chherchherra and Nakta-Nakti skits are also in a way the humourous drama forms. Bhatra Nat is a fully developed traditional theatre in Baster.

In plains of Chhattisgarh we find two fully developed theatre forms; one is Rahas and another is Nautcha. Rahas again is a traditional theatre based on the childhood adventures of Lord Krishna. This is Chhattisgarhi version of Rasa-Lila. Nautcha is very secular theatre evolved and developed in the rural peasantry of this region. Unlike some other theatre forms of North India Hindi belt like Nautanki, Swang, Match and Turra Kalangi, the nautcha has been originated in the peasants whereas all other theatre forms mentioned above are only partly related with the rural peasantry. The contribution of the elite to the nautcha form is insignificant.

The origin of nautcha into a developed theatre form is not very old. The dramatic form has originated in this region with the Maratha invasion in the later part of the eighteenth century. This area fell to Marathas when Bimbaji Rao Bhonsle while going to attack Orissa, also attacked Ratanpur, the headquarters of Southern Kalchuri kingdom and occupied it. Marathas after establishing their right on the region have posted their officers at Bilaspur and Raipur to administer the area and collect revenue. Malgujaris were given to Maratha Sardars and their brahmin 'amins' and officials to honour their bravery. In the early nineteenth century a large population of Marathas and Maharashtrian Brahmins had come to Chhattisgarh and settled down here. With the Maratha army also came the entertainers, musicians and performers.

'Gamatta' word is used for humour and entertainment in Marathi. The entertainers used to perform dance and drama to entertain the Maratha soldiers, army Sardars and officials. The female performers used to perform dances and the male performers the humourous skits and music. This had evolved in to 'gammatta' and 'tamasha' in Marathi land. Gammatta is also a very essential part of Chhattisgarhi 'nautcha' which is some times a part of the play and some times used only as a humourous filler to entertain the audience to give a pause. In the beginning there would have been only 'gammata' and from their would have evolved 'nautcha' as a full fledged theatre form.

Ganda musicians have also contributed allot to the development of nautcha theatre. Ganda is a low caste of musicians who form the musical bands and perform in the marriages especially of the rural folk of the region. Up to some twenty five years back the marriage parties used to stay for four to five days and these Ganda musicians also used to stay with them. The band parties had two 'nishan' players (drummers), one 'dhapda' playe, one mohari (local shahanai) player, one timki player and minimum one or two natchkars(dancers). The natchkars are always male who make up and dress up as female. These dancers accompany the band party and dance on the tune. After the lunch and dinner the marriage party members had a lot of time and leisure, and in a rural setting it is quite boring to stay for days together in a village without doing any thing. So they used to invite the nachakar to entertain them. The nachkar in his dance performance used to present mimes of the women in general with obscene and exaggerated gestures. They also used to produce mimicry and mimes of the important members both male and female of both the families of the bride and bridegroom to create humour to entertain the members of the marriage party. For such humourous performances they were rewarded by the party members. Even to day the natchkars are the greatest source of humour and entertainment in the village marriages. If there were two natchkars one would mime as a female and the other as a male. In their conversation they will create humourous situations dramatically with their robust sence of humour. In the early phase of the evolution of nautcha these ganda dancers have contributed much to develop and enrich the nautcha theatre through their music, mimes and mimicry.

The organisation of nautcha party is simple. Any theatre loving person or performer would take initiative to organise a nautcha troupe. He would identify some boys who are interested in the theatre activity, music and entertainment. The convener generally becomes the organiser and forms a dramatic group. They collect some money amongst themselves and from the villagers to meet the primary expenses.

The dramatic performance is simple. The group would select some topic and immediately start working on the subject as a workshop. There is no written script and no definite dialogues. While preparing the drama they will develop the dramatic situations, the scenes and the dialogues. In each performance they would go on improvising the play. So the wo performances are never alike and the same. The nautcha is basically a theatre of humour and satire in which the rural dramatists take up only such subjects which are of immediate concern to them and on which they can laugh at and make comments by satire and sarcasm. Originally the male and female both the parts were performed by the male artists. Even to day the female part is done by the male artist in so many troupes. But since about last thirty years or so, some girls have also started participating in the nautcha.

In the beginning of the twentieth century a section of the malguzars were attracted towards the nautcha, as by that time it became an important means of entertainment in the rural life of Chhattisgarh. Some of the malgujars used to invite Dewar girls for dance performances at the time of some function like marriage celebration or celebration on childbirth. They were also invited to perform dances at the village madais (fares). The feudal decadence was also reflected in these malguzars who used to imitate the big zamindars and Rajas life style. Some rich malguzars used to invite the dancing girls from Laknow, Benaras and Calcutta for mujra. Those who could not afford to invite dancing girls from outside used to invite Dewar girls for the same purpose. The poverty striken Dewars also started imitating the dancing girls who used to come from outside. This is how a relationship between the malguzars and the Dewar girls had developed. When some enlightened malguzars became interested in the nautcha theatre, they induced these Dewar girls in the theatre activity.

Nautcha is a complete play and gammatta a part of it. Gammatta is humourous skit used as a filler in the intervals. In all the folk theatre forms of north India, dances and skits are used as fillers to break the monotony and give time to the artists to take some rest. The spectators also feel relaxed due to this diversion. In nautcha also there are two types of diversions. One is completely humourous Gammat Skit and the other is "Jokkad-Pari" performance. Themes in the gammattas are generally woven around the innocent villagers and their ignorance about the wordly things, the rurals attitude towards the urbans. They make satirical comments on those rurals who have deserted them and have joined the urbanes. They are laughed at in both the societies. They also make humourous and satirical comments on every aspect of their day-to-day life. To laugh at others is easy but to laugh at ownself requires courage and robust sense of humour. Indian villager in his worst hardships and economic conditions can do it with his very developed sence of humour. That is why he can stand against all the odds of life.

In 'Jokkad Pari' which is also called nachkaudi scenes one handsome boy dresses like a 'pari' or fairy. The concept of 'pari' is quite different than the fairy concept with wings and vested with mystic and supernatural powers. Here 'Pari' symbolises as a beautiful and good noble woman. Now again it is interesting to note that though the female artists have started participating in the nautcha, but in the 'Jokkad Pari' episode only a male artist becomes a 'Pari'.

The Jokkads who are generally in a pair with oil torches in their hands first occupy the stage. The musicians accompanists also come and sit on the left corner of the stage. The conception of jokkads is not the same as of a joker in circus or a clown in an English Drama or a Vidushak of a Sanskrit Classic or Sangitak. Here a jokkad is an entertainer who knows singing and dancing and he is witty, humourous and full of life. He can converse with the Pari in such an innocent and pure humour, that he can make everybody laugh. The Pari makes her entrance from the audience with gaudy and catchy make up. She always keeps a 'lota' (water jug) on her head and walks and talks like delicate housewife. Both the Jokkads and the Pari converse wittily and just when the humourous situation is created, start dancing. Jokkads start dancing with the mashals (torches) in their hands and the Pari with the lota on her head dances vigourously without holding it. Now a days though due to the electrification in most of the villages the oil torches are not required, but even then the sticks are kept in hands by the Jokkads as without it they can feel some thing missing without which they can not perform. The quick witted conversation of the Joker and Pari keep the audience laughing all the time.

In last twenty five years I have seen a number of nautcha performances in Raipur, Durg and Bilaspur districts of Chhattisgarh. They are generally on social problems such as the plight of a husband of two wives whose life is always unsteady like a pipal leaf, or an innocent son of a farmer who is dragged to vices by a spoiled companion who ultimately suffers from leprosy for his sins. In one nautcha the theme was 'Bharam Ke Bhoot' means the ghost created out of illusions. This play is full of humour but at the same time it is a satire on the superstitions and backwardness. 'Ponga Pandit' is another nautcha in which an innocent farmer and illitrate Brahmin have been depicted humourously. "Gaon Ke Nam Sasural More Nam Damad" (The name of the village is my in-laws house and my name is son-in-law) is full of humour. This play has also been adopted by Habib Tanvir. Mr. Tanvir has also staged some modern plays and Sanskrit classics in the nautcha style.

The nautcha has been originated from nachya character of Marathi Gammatwho mimes as a female character, that is why it is called nautcha. Every character makes his entry with dance steps. The costumes are simple and the stage is an open courtyard or a platform. The musicians sit in the left corner on the backside and the audience in the front. There are no wings and no curtains. The costumes and make-up is simple. Wigs, beards and mustaches are also used but no masks are used. Generally in the village set-up courtyard or a varanda of a near by house is used as a green room. White soap stone and clay, turmeric powder, pink and red colours and lipstick are used in the make-up.

First of all two dancers, one male and another female enter into the stage. They worship the lord Ganesh and Goddess Sarswati to bless them for the success of the naucha. After that they also worship the local deities Maoli, Kankalin, Bamlai and Saranggarhin etc. This is the 'purva rang' of the nautcha. After the worship the stage is left by the dancers and the play starts.

I am describing here one nautcha play which I have seen and recorded recently. The contents are like this: a rich and young farmer who is married is an innocent person. His wife is a very religious woman who always reads Tulsikrit Ramayan as and when free. She is regarded as a noble, kind hearted and religious woman, hence respected by all other women in the village.

One bad character of the village conspires to induce and drag the rich peasant to vices. He offers him mahua liquor in the beginning and gradually introduces him to gambling, meat eating, regular boozing. They also visit the dancing girls and prostitutes. His fields become barron due to neglect and his total wealth is spent up including the ornaments of his wife. He becomes completely broke. When his wife objects to his extravagance he turns her out of the house. The lady went to a temple in a near by village with his holy book and starts reciting Ramayan before the women folk of the village.

The bad character develops leprosy and his wife rebukes and blames for his sins. She takes him to the holy river for a dip. On the bank of the river in the very temple when they enter they found the religious wife of the innocent peasant. They both pray to forgive them for their sins. The peasant who was insulted by the prostitute was also driven out. He was hungry and thirsty and had no money to buy food. He decides to commit suicide and comes to the river at the same place. Finding his wife and his bad character friend, he also regrets for his sins. Both of them take a dip in the river and when advised to touch the holy book Ramayan with the forehead, the leprosy is cured and all of them again return to their own village to start a fresh.

In the beginning of this paper I have called the nautcha as a theatre of peasantry. The themes of the nautcha are taken from the rural every day problems. The artistes also belong to peasantry. Everyone has some land holding small or big. Generally the artists are marginal farmers. In the monsoon season they work on their fields or as farm labourers and after the harvest they become busy with the nautcha. Nautcha troupes are not professional at the best they can be called semi professionals. They partly depend on the agriculture and partly on the nautcha. At the time of madai (village fares), marriages, Ganesh festivals and other such occasions, the nautcha troupes are invited to perform. They are paid from three hundred to one thousand to five thousand rupees as remuneration.

The outstanding artists of nautcha in this century have been Thakur Ram, Lalu Ram, Madan Nishad, Ram Lal, Dwarka,

Bhulwaram, Amar Singh, Fida bai, Mala Bai, Kismet Bai and Ganeshram Nyayik das, Jhumuk lal and Phirturam. Shri Habib Tanvir, Dau Mahasing Chandrakar, Shri Ramchandra Deshmukh, and Laxman Chandrakar are some theatre persons who have done some new experiments in nautcha gener. They have also worked hard to promote the nautcha theatre but it has resulted into deviation and modernisation.Though nautcha is only about one hundred years old theatre form in which it has developed into a complete theatre form. In the early twentieth century, it has become quite deep rooted in the rural Chhattisgarh. Any effort to make it urbane is not acceptable to its traditional audience. It should be left free from any outside interference and allowed to grow spontaneously.

Naucha performance of H. Maypuri

The musicians enter on the stage and occupy the left corner and arrange their sitting and musical instruments. Then the jokkad enters from oneside along with two najaias. The jokkad is holding stick in his hand. All of them start dancing and singing prayer for lord Ganesh. After this they also sing a hymn for Sarswati the goddess of learning. In the end they sing a hymn in which they after their prayer to all the local gods and goddesses like Maoli, Telgin, Bamlai Samilal, Dongargarhin, Saranggarhin, Thakur Deo and Budha Deo. The musical ensemble play on their instruments and some of them also give company in the singing of prayer. This is how the purvarang of Naucha is performed.

After the completion of the purvarang one old man enters. He is wearing white clothes and a waistcoat. He is keeping a long scarf on his shoulder and wearing a turban which shows that he is a respectable person of his village. He has also applied a sandalwood paste mark on his forehead, which indicates that he is a religious person. He sits on a mattress. One wooden box is kept in which he keeps his account books and money. Actually he is a landlord and also a moneylander of that village. He is also very miser. He opens the wooden box and worships the goddess Laxmi with folded hands and then closes the lid and puts a lock on it. In the mean time his wife and his only young son enters. He looks at them curiously.

He spoke thus to his son. O my obedient son, go and take a round of the paddy fields. See whether the servants are working properly or not. The son goes. One poor person enters with folded hands and wish him, "Ram Ram Dauji". "Ram Ram brother." How are you? Why have you come at this time?" Dau (respectful address) I am in need of some money. Please land me one hundred rupees. I will return it after the harvest."

"You will have to return me two hundred rupees after the harvest then only I can give you the money." Poor farmer, "But this is too much. This is unjust."

Dau, "Then you can go and borrow the money from somebody else."

Poor farmer, "No no Dau! Dont do like that. Where else can I go! Please land me money. I will return your money with your desired rate of interest.

The money lander counts money and gives the farmer only ninety rupees instead of one hundred. When the poor man counts he finds that those were only ninety rupees. He looks at the land lord and says,

"These are only ninety rupees"

"Yes! Ten rupees I have deducted as interest."

The poor fellow puts his signature on his cashbook and leaves. The landlord puts his hand in his shirt's pocket and takes out some coins. He counts them several times and then found that twenty five naya paisa coin was short. He tries to search it in all the pockets of his shirt, then on the mattress. He picks his scarf and twitched it. Then he rolls on his mattress and tries to find out the coin. His wife was looking at him curiously and asked,

"What are you looking for?"

"My one fore anna coin is missing. I am searching it.

"Let it go, but dont behave like this. I dont like all this. If some one will see you rolling like this on the floor for a chawanni what will they think of us."

"How can I let it go. I have amassed wealth by collecting each penny!"

Then he again starts searching the coin with his funny actions singing a song. By his acting and funny dance and gestures he creates comic situation and the audience responds with laughter. His wife also dances with him mocking at him for his miserness.

The scene changes. The landlord and his wife leaves the stage. Their son enters. He takes a few rounds of the stage with fast steps as if he is going some where with an urgent work. A saint with long hair, beard and moustaches enters. He is wearing saffron coloured clothes. He is also holding a kamandal (water jar) in his hand. He is reciting a song.

This world is a Mayapuri
All the relations in this world are selfish.
Neither the mother, nor the father
Nor the wife, nor any other
Are true relations?
All the relations are superfluous
All the relations are based on 'Maya'

The boy wished the saint with folded hands, "Ram Ram." "Ram Ram" replied the saint and asked him "Where are you going so hurriedly?"

"I am going to inspect my fields. My father has asked me to do so."

The saint, "But why should you obey your father so sincerely?"

"Why! Why should I not obey him?

He is my father after all. What ever he says, it is in my interest. He loves me so much.

"Sad Guru, Sad Guru," the saint, murmurs.

O my son! You are mistaken. This world is a Maya Puri. It is guided by Maya Maya is a great thing. All the relations in this world are selfish. So spend some time in the prayer of god, the almighty. Spend some time in Satsang (company of saints)"

What do you talk! All the relations are selfish! How can it be?

My father loves me so much! My mother loves me so much! My wife loves me so much that she even does not eat without seeing my face!"

No, no my son! This is all fallacious. You are in illusion. If you want, you can yourself examine it."

O saint you are talking some thing, which is new to me. I will surely like to examine, but tell me how to do it?"

O my son! come with me. You do whatever I suggest you to do. You pretend as if a snake has bitten you. I will take you on my shoulders to your house and then you will experience how much your family members love you!"

The scene of the land lords house where that landlord is sitting on his chair in the courtyard of the house. The landlady is talking sweetly with him offering him a glass of water. The saint enters with the unconscious body of the landlord's son on his back.

"Sad Guru, Sad Guru, Narayan...Narayan...
"Ram Ram O old saint! Land lord addresses.

"Ram Ram sahukar (money lander). Here is your son. A cobra has bitten him on his way to paddy fields. He has become unconscious, so I have brought him here."

All the family members, the father, mother, his sister and his wife all of them surround the unconscious body of the boy and start weeping loudly. Every one of them is crying. The body is lying on the ground in the courtyard. Suddenly the landlord turns towards the saint and requests him to do some thing to save his son's life.

"You are a saint a religious person. You people possess supernatural powers. You can definitely save my son's life. Please save his life. I am prepared to do any thing for him."

Saint closes his eyes and murmurs some sacred words as if he is remembering some super natural power then he opens his eyes and says,

"Yes his life can be saved, provided someone is prepared to give his life for him." So now tell me who will give his life. I have religious water in my kamandal. Who so ever will drink this water will die and this boy's life will be saved.

Land lord looks at all the persons one by one to read the feelings of everyone. Then he says to his wife, "You are his dear mother! You loved him so much! So you drink this holy water from the kamandal and save your son!" The lady thinks for a while and then said, "Why should I die. I have still many duties to perform. I have also to go to Badrinath and Jagannath Puri for pilgrimage. I will not give my life." Then she looks at her husband and said, "You have done everything in your life, enjoyed all the pleasures. Why dont you give your life for your dear son?"

"No! no! How can I give my life? I have still many things to do. I have loaned a lot of money to the people. I have to recover it. Then I have to take care of my belongings, which I have amassed with great efforts. How can I giveup my life." Then he looks towards his servant and asks him, "O Budhru my dear obedient servant! You have always been helping me. Please also help me now. You do not have any body as your own relative. You have neither a wife nor children. So please drink the holy water and save my son. You owe me ten rupees also. Although I dont want you to die, because I will lose that money. But for the sake of my son's life, I will forget about the money. Please drink the holy water and save my son. Budhru is perplexed. He thinks for a while and then said,

"O Dauji, I have not enjoyed all the pleasures of life. I am not yet married and do not know what is the pleasure of a family life. If I die like that I will become a ghost. So Dauji! I will not drink the holy water from the saint's kamandal."

Then the landlord tells his daughter to drink the holy water and save her brother. She is a married woman. Her father tells the saint to offer her the holy water from his kamandal. The girl spoke to her father,

"Now I am married and I belong to someone else. How can I

give my life for your son? I am not concerned about his life. Why dont one of you people sacrifice your life for your dear son? You were always boasting that you loved him so much, then why dont you sacrifice. You both are old and have enjoyed all the pleasures of life."

The father was unhappy hearing all these words. He said,

"I am prepared to give my life but who will look after my wealth. If this is wasted then all my life will go waste." Then he calls his daughter-in-law, and spoke to her,

"O daughter-in-law! see your husband's life is in danger. You love your husband so dearly and you are a virtuous wife. You drink the holy water from the saint's kamadal and save his life. By your sacrifice god will give you a place in heaven."

The daughter-in-law started crying and spoke thus,

"O father-in-law I am too young to die. It is true that I loved him so much, but now if he dies how can I help! I am still young and can remarry with someone else and enjoy my life. What is the fun in giving life for a person whose life is ending?"

When the saint heard everybody's words, he spoke thus,

"O land lord, listen! The lives of all of you are precious, but I am a saint. I have no purpose to live. Neither I have any property to look after, nor I can marry someone. So if you wish, I can give my life to save your son's life."

Hearing the saint's words all of them became happy and said the landlord, "O grand old saint! You are so generous and so kind to us! Please drink the holy water quickly and save my son's life."

The wife of the landlord and the daughter-in-law both touched the feet of the saint and spoke thus,

"O great saint please hurry up. Drink the holy water. God will surely give you a place in the heaven. Drink the holy water from the kamandal." Listening all of these words the saint smiled with sarcasm. He murmured Narayan...Narayan... and drank the water from his kamandal. As soon as he drank the water the boy got up murmuring Narayan...Narayan...Narayan...All his family members rushed towards him. The father and mother both cried, "O dear son where were you going leaving us here."

His wife caught his feet and cried, "O my beloved husband, how could I live without you in this cruel world!" Then the boy spoke thus,

I have heard all of you. All these relations are untrue. I am neither your son nor you are my parents. Then he told his wife, "I am not your husband nor you are my wife. I have known the mystery of life. This world is a Maya Puri. All the relations are selfish here so I am leaving you all. The boy got up and touched the feet of the saint.

A Nautcha Play

This nautcha play has been recorded by Pisi Lal Yadav, editor of Madai for Madhya Pradesh Adivasi Lokkala Parishad, Bhopal. The theme of the play is based on the family partition between two brothers. They play in its beginning is full of pathos but in the later part it has a lot of element of humour. There are only five characters in this play–

Characters

(1) **Gountar** – Village cultivator and elder brother
(2) **Phoolbati** – Gountar's wife
(3) **Babulal** – Gountar's younger brother
(4) **Mangal** – A villager
(5) **Gangotri** – Babulal's wife

Phoolbati : O father of Ramau listen to me.

Gountar : Yes.

Phoolbati : Tell your younger brother to bring a new lugra (sari) for me as all my clothes have worn out. Both of them wife and husband are always wearing new clothes.

Gountar : Don't tell me all this when I am taking meals. You ladies always talk such things at the meals time!

Phoolbati : O my mother! What did I tell you? I will use the same sari, but should the children remain naked! You always talk like this and to avoid.

Gountar : Could you not tell all this at any other time? You always start telling your Ramayana (problems) at the meals time!

Phoolbati : This simple talk becomes unpleasant to you!

Gountar : Oh! You have felt it. You are a simpleton. You are so touchy! They are educated. They move in such company that is why they have to put on nice clothes. If they will not wear good clothes then who else, shall wear! We work in the field and do our agricultural duty. O. K. You tell him, he will bring a sari for you also.

Phoolbati : I am not worried about me but I am asking about our children.

Gountar : He will purchase clothes for the children don't be sad.

Phoolbati : We are working so hard like bulls and baffalows and worried even for a penny and they are spending good amount ofmoney on eating and on new clothes. How do you feel good about it? You have handed over every thing to them, are we their servants?

Gountar : What has happened to you? How are you talking so unwisely? Babulal is educated, how can we compare us with him. We are Gobar Ganesh (foolish) before him, ha...ha...ha...

Phoolbati : Whatever I tell you, you laugh away. You will have to repent one day.

Gountar : Oh! What is there to worry about it! If younger brother and his wife will not enjoy in his elder brother's and his wife's home then how can they enjoy? When Babulal will come, you tell him to purchase sari and clothes for you, he will do. I am going towards the field.

Gountar leaves after meals.

Phoolbati : O younger brother...

Babulal : What happened?

Phoolbati : The clothes of children and my sari are worn out. You purchase these clothes for us. When I told your brother he has told me to ask you for this.

Babulal : See sister-in-law! How I am managing the family expences , I only know this difficulty. The debt of the sahukar still not cleared and you people are desiring for new clothes.

Phoolbati : Oh! Why will you sell paddy? We will remain without new clothes. You people are wearing everytime new clothes. Your children are wearing terricott clothes and our children are not having even coarse clothes to wear.

Babulal : See sister-in-law! Don't talk like this creating differences among us.

Phoolbati : You are differentiating, not we. How long can we tolerate. Are we your servants? What ever you give us we will eat and wear, as if you are the owner of everything.

Babulal : O sister-in-law hold your tongue otherwise I will not tolerate....

Phoolbati : What can you do? Will you beat me? You are eating sweets and dry fruits in your room and we are craving even for puffed rice and gram.

Babulal : You also eat sweets and dry fruits. You are creating malice.

Phoolbati : Malice you are creating. For your children you are giving him motichur ladu (a kind of sweet prepration) and for our children parched rice. If you are really wise and responsible then treat every one equally.

Gangotri : You are becoming jealous of my children of their good eating and wearing. Let your eyes be blind.

Phoolbati : You should become blind. If you could give one ladu (sweet) to my child what would you lose? You are driving him away as if he is a dog.

Gangotri : Allright we wont give him. Why should we give. You also purchase and give your child to eat. Talking like a rich woman!

Phoolbati : You are rich! You are the owner, you are the master!.

Gangotri : Yes! I am the owner due to my husband. Did you bring riches from your father's home?

Phoolbati : If others would have brought, I would also have brought. Did you bring from your father's and brother's home cart load of wealth. Don't behave like a owner of all this.

Gangotri : Don't talk like this. Don't name my father and brother in this matter, otherwise...

Phoolbati : Otherwise what will you do ...?

Gangotri : I will beat you hard and flay your skin. I will not consider relationship of sister-in-law any more. How dare you talk about my father and brother?

Phoolbati : Let him come. You will exaggerate for this? How much can we tolerate you people? You have kept us starved.

Gangotri : Have you not eaten, are you starved o liar!.

Phoolbati : Liar you are, foul mouth you are. You are speaking as if hurling knieves and daggers.

Gangotri : You are calling me a liar then you are a thief, a liar.

Phoolbati : Yes, if you will talk like this then I will also reply you in the same coin. How dare you call me a liar, a thief. You are a liar, you are a theif.

Gangotri : This harlot is calling me a thief. I will not stay in this house for a minute... onha.. ha and starts weeping.

Babulal : (To Gangotri) Be silent, we have suffered a lot, we have heard enough. Today we will finally decide whether we live in this house or they live.

Gangotri : I will not stay here. You divide every thing today only, otherwise I am going to my mother's place (She pretends as if going).

Babulal : Oh! Keep patience, let my brother come, we will force him for having a partition. (Gountar arrives)

Gountar : What has happened? When I come I find you people quarreling.

Babulal : Listen brother now our rice can not be coocked together. We can not eat from the same pot. You give us our share.

Gountar : Listen o brother! Wherever four utensils are kept together, they make sound naturally. Stop this quarrel, its not good.

Gangotri : We will not live together. Give us our share. If you don't give us our share then we will construct a hut any where else and live there.

Gountar : Are Rama!... Rama!!... Do not talk like this o sister-in-law. Which family does not have such quarrels. Avoid this quarrel.

Babulal : No brother we don't want to live with you. Give us our share just now.

Gountar : Listen Laxmi (riches) also comes with good thinking and Laxmi goes away with wrong thinking. Don't be angry. Why do you speak such thing O Phoolbati?

Phoolbati : I have not done any thing. I have only said to bring a sari for me. After that these people have created this fuss.

Babulal : No brother, we don't want to quarrel with you, that will creat pain in our stomach. Let us have partition. That is the only solution to finish this quarrel, otherwise... otherwise...

Gountar : Are Rama!... Rama!!... Don't talk like this brother. If you wish to have partition, want to eat separately then bring some person from the village who can mediate. I do not want to be unfair.

Babulal : I will not call anybody, you are elder so you do it and do the partition.

Gountar : All right if I am elder then why call anybody. What are the things you want to have, you can take and whatever you will give me, I will accept and be satisfied.

Babulal : Have you that much satisfaction?

Gountar : Yes brother, I will be satisfied.

Babulal : All right, then listen, the veranda is yours and the rooms are mine.

Gountar : I accept this proposal.

Babulal : The grain bin is yours and the rice is mine.

Gountar : All right.

Babulal : The munga tree is yours and the fruits are mine.

Gountar : All right, All right.

Babulal : The blanket, bed carpet are yours in the daytime and they are mine in the night.

Gountar : This also I accept.

Phoolbati : (To her husband) What has happened to you? Are you agreeing for all his demands without thinking.

Gountar : You need not worry.

Babulal : The front partition of the cow and she buffalo are yours and the back portion is mine.

Gountar : This also is accepted.

Babulal : The utensils while cooking are mine and at the time of cleaning they are yours.

Gountar : This also I accept. You be happy.

Babulal : Gangotri are you hearing.

Gangotri : You have done a fine job. They are showing great satisfaction. When they will starve then only they will realize our importance.

Babulal : Let us celebrate this occasion. Cook khir, bara, bhajia all festival dishes. We got what ever we desired. Also invite our friends. My sister-in-law will be jealous to see all this.

Phoolbati : I advised you not to accept this sort of partition but you succumbed to the designs of those cheats, those conspirators.

Gountar : Don't call them cheats and conspirators. He is my younger brother. Let them be happy.

Phoolbati : If I don't call them cheats then what shall I do. They are murderers, due to them our small children are starving.

Gountar : Don't worry god will help us also.

Phoolbati : What will the god do? You are destroying everything. We are lying in the Veranda and in the rooms they are sleeping in comfort. They are eating rice from the bin, shall we lick the earth of the bin. We will irrigate the tree and they will eat the fruits. Without the bedding and spreads outs and coverings we will sleep in the cold and they will sleep with all the comforts. We will feed the cattle and they will take the milk. They will eat in the utensils and we will clean them. Are we their servants? What sort of is this partition? Have anybody heard about such partition anywhere in the world? You have become stupid in love of your brother!

Gountar : You are right. I could never think that they will do all this, but to whatever I have agreed I will accept. God will do justice.

Mangal : Rama... Rama... brother. Please sit down. Why are you both sitting quietly.

Gountar : What can I tell you brother ! You must have heard about our family partition.

Mangal : Yes, I have come to know and I am surprised. What sort of partition is this?

Phoolbati : Ar.... the saw cuts the throat of the simpleton! He is behaving like a fool. Always says yes... Yes for every thing does not work. Loss and benefit have to be considered, is not it Mangal babu?

Mangal : Yes, sister-in-law. By keeping mum it wont do. Let us find out some way. Babulal is a killer, he has cut your throat.

Gountar : What shall I do, I am not able to think. You suggest some remedy, some way.

Mangal : Ok, then listen to me. (He whispers in his ear). Will this idea work?

Gountar : Yes brother, your idea is fine. I will follow it.

Mangal : Sister-in-law you also listen (he whispers something in Phoolbati's ear also)

(Babulal is coming from outside)

Gountar : Ar!... this Veranda is mine. Don't put your feet on it.

Babulal : If I do not walk on the veranda floor, how can I enter in the rooms?

Gountar : I will not allow you to put yours feet on veranda. You may jump or gamolas, but will not walk through the veranda. That is mine.

Babulal : This is absurd. Brother let me walk through the veranda.

(Babulal is ascending on the grain bin)

Gountar : Don't ascend on the bin, this is mine.

Babulal : Without ascending how can I take out rice from it?

Gountar : I have told you that the bin is mine. I will not allow you to ascend on it. If you will insist I will break your legs. (Babulal is climbing on the munga tree).

Gountar : Again you are doing mischief. This tree is mine. If you climb on the tree I will not tolerate. I will pull your leg, which may break.

Babulal : Without climbing on the tree how can I pluck the fruits. Brother please let me climb the tree.

Gountar : No.. No.. I will not allow you to climb on the tree. The tree is mine.

Babulal : O God! I have fallen in my own trap.

Gountar tells Phoolbati - Put all the beds coverings, blankets in water.

Phoolbati : But why so..

Gountar : Now you will see the fun. You just dip them all in water.

(Phoolbati dips all the bed sheets, blankets and all other coverings in the water)

Babulal comes in the evening to Gountar and tell him–

Brother it is sunset now. Give me beds, blankets and other coverings for the night, as par agreement. In the night time they are mine. Gountar gives him all the wet beds and coverings. Take them

Babulal : Oh! These are wet. Why have you done so. Now how can we used them. What will do how can we in the night.

Gountar : Whatever you like, you do. In the day time they are mine. I will do whatever I like. I may dip them in water or put them in the sunshine.

(Babulal comes and starts milking the cow.)

Gountar beating the cow on head and face with a stick.

Babulal : Are!... re!!... why are you beating the cow? It is not allowing me to milk.

Gountar : It's not eating and drinking. The front portion of the cow is mine so I can do anything I like with it.

Babulal falls on his feet and says– Pardon me brother, selfishness made me blind. I dug a pit for you but I have myself fallen in it. Please pardon me brother, please...

Gountar : On the evil advice of your wife you are not my brother. You are my enemy of my some previous life.

Babulal : No brother. I touch your feet, please pardon me. Now I have realized. I have learned a lesson.

Mangal : Babulal how clever are you? You have cheated your god like brother, don't you feel ashamed of your act?

Then he turns towards Gangotri and said– Now you sister-in-law celebrate this festively. Prepare sweet, meats and other tasty dishes. You are also not ashamed of your shameful act and evil designs. By studying two words you think you have become intelligent?

Gangotri : Please pardon me. I also became blind due to selfishness.

Mangal : Touch the feet of your elder sister-in-law and pray for pardon. Babulal, if you want a partition you call some senior persons of the village to mediate and also offer your brother the right of elderliness. Do you understand you selfish fellow!

Babulal : No brother, now we will not like to be separated. We will live together with our brother and work with them and earn our living in a moral way.

Mangal : What do you say Gountar brother?

Gountar : I have no malice in my heart. I have no objection neither today nor tomorrow.

Mangal : All right live a moral life with good intentions and do hard work. There is heaven in the moral thinking and heard work.

CHAPTER 16

Pandwani

Pandwani is a traditional theatre form of Chhattisgarh. It is based on the theme of Mahabharat. Pandwani means Pandawa + Vani which means the legend of Pandawas. The genesis of Pandwani is in the Pardhan Gond legend. The name Pandwani is originally of this Pardhan Gond legend which is like a tribal epic based on the great epic Mahabharat but with several differences. It has incorporated many. Gond myths and sociological aspects of the Gond society. The Pandwani legend is in verse which runs in about four hundred pages. The main emphasis of this ballad is on the valour of Pandwas who defeated Korawas in the battle of Kurukshetra known as Mahabharat. The hero of Pandwani is Bhima and neither Yudhshthira nor Arjun.

Pardhan Gonds are ballad singers and are bards of the Gond tribe. There are some more legends of epic character in their narratives, they are 'Gondwani', 'Ramayani' and 'Karamseni'. They also narrate the genealogy of the Gond rulers and their septs. They also narrate the legend of 'Lingo Pen' the great Gond god from whom the tribe derives its origin. In all these legends which are in verse form the combination of history, religion, myths and sociological aspects are blended so poetically, that they have achieved the epic level. Dr. T.B. Niak who was the director of the Madhya Pradesh Tribal Research Institute got some of these legends documented. Shekh Gulab who was a school teacher in a tribal school documented Pandwani, Gondwani and Ramayani for the institute and they were published under the editorship of Dr. T.B. Naik.

Pardhan bards used to travel distant place to visit their traditional hosts after the Kharif harvest throughout Gondwana, which spread from Vindhyachal to Godawari and from Chandrapur in Vidarbha to Sambalpur in Orissa. This is how there legends spread all over the Gondwana land. Dewar is another nomadic community whose origin is also from the Mandla tribal region. According to Stephen Fuchs the community is a branch of Bhumia tribe and the Bhumia tribe is originally a branch of Baiga tribe but both Dewar and Bhumia prefer to call themselves as sub tribes of Gonds.[1] Verrier Elwin considers the Dewar community of Chhattisgarh a mixed caste of Gond and Kanwar. [2] They lived in Chhattisgarh and are small tribe of musicians. They also sing the ballads Gondwani, Pandwani, ramayani and other songs on a small sarangi. There is a great similarity in the ballads of Pardhans and Dewars and the way of singing. A group of Dewars had migrated to Ratanpur the capital town of Kalchuri branch of Chhattisgarh and from there they had spread all over chhattisgarh. As nomad bards they spread the ballads Pandwani, Gondwani and Ramayani to all over Chhattisgarh.

Nomenclature of Mahabharat as Pandwani is established by the Pardhans and Dewars through their ballad. Initially it was in ballad form. Now Pandwani is a popular mono theatre form. The word Pandwani means the legend of Pandwas. Mahabharat and Ramayana are two great epics of India which have inspired several art forms. Mahabharata is considered the fifth Veda, that itself establishes its importance in Indian society.

Indian Society was divided in to four categories which were called "Varanas", the 'Bhahmanas', 'Kshatrias', 'Vaishas' and 'Shudras'. Education and learning were the sole domain of

---

1. *The Gonds and Bhumia of Eastern Mandla,* Stephen Fuchs, p. 199
2. *The Baiga,* V. Elwin, p. 343

Barhamans, the country from the invaders, the duty of the Vaishnavas was to make the country economically self sufficient and powerful through agriculture and trade and duty of the Shudras was to serve the country through their service and craftsmanship. Then there were untouchables who were known as 'Antajyas'. The Shudras and Antajyas were not allowed to be educated. Reading of religious book such as 'Vedas', 'Puranas' and other religious scriptures was almost a monopoly of Brahamins.

Before the invention writing of paper the books were scarce and were written on 'bhojpatras' and 'tadpatras' (palm leaf). The number of such books were very little and they were not available easily, hence they were memorized. This practice was called 'Smriti'. The tradition of 'Smriti' practice is very significant aspect of Indian oral tradition. All the great scriptures including Vedas, Samhitas, Upnishadas and even epics like Mahabharata which has more than a lac 'Slokas' (Verses) were in oral tradition(Smriti).

The Shudras were debared from reading, writing but were also listening the religious discourse (pravachan) of these scriptures. Due to such strong rules probably a parallel stream of narrative style developed amongst the common folk in which the texts of the Sanskrit scriptures become narratives in 'Bhasha', the language of the common folk. This became possible because of the skill of the bards, who existed even in the ancient times. The 'Suta', 'Kushilava' and 'Gandarva' are some such communities which have been mentioned in old texts. There are several narrative forms which are based on the texts of Mahabharata and Ramayana which are spread all over the country. These narratives have been developed mostly by non Brahmins, mostly from lower castes of bards. The discourse of religious book was strictly the monopoly of the Brahmins and the listeners were the 'Dwijas' (the three higher castes Brahamins, Kshatriyas and Vaishas). Due to such restrictions the talented bards were inspired to develop a parallel style of narratives based on these texts.

There are several narratives which are based on Mahabharat

such as Pandunkakada of Mewat are, Burrakatha of Andhra Pradesh, Harikatha of Karnataka and Andhra and Pandwani of Gondwana which comprises of Mahakosal and Chhattisgarh. All these forms have been developed by non-Brahmians and lower castes anc are popular amongst the common folk. Pandwani is performed by Pardhans who are bards of the Gonds. It is a small community and greatly influenced by Hindu religion. They have come in close contact of Hindu culture in last about a century and largely Hinduised. Pardhan is a sub division of Gond tribe but they are only about four percent of the Gonds in population. Their main habitat is in the Satpura hilly region of alluvial land of river Narmada. They are also found scattered all over central India wherever the Gonds live. Shyam Rao Hiwale has done a fine monograph on the community, "The Pardhans of the upper Narmada and Valley", which was published in the year 1945 with a forward by Dr. V. Elwin.

According to Shyam Rao Hiwale Pardhan is the younger brother of Gond tribe and hence they have an important place in the larger Gond tribe "They have always sung the songs of the heroic deeds of the Gond rulers and their glorious history".[1]

The balled of Pardhans is mainly based on Mahabharat epic but the Pardhans have assimilated several Gond myths and sociological aspects of their own in it brilliantly. The main characters of Mahabharata find place in Pandwani also but they have been presented skillfull blanding of Gond hero's characteristics and qualities. The hero of Mahabharata is Arjuna but in Pandwani the hero is Bhima. He is the strongest than any other character of Mahabharata and with his robust commonsense he is able to avert all the calamities faced by Pandwas and could defeat all their enemies. The name of Kunti the mother of Pandwa brothers is Kotama and the name of Gandhari the mother of Korwas is Gandari in Pandwani. Pandwas are one hundred brothers according

1. The Pardhans of the Upper Narmada & Valley, Shyam Rao Hiwale.

to Mahabharata but they are twenty-one brothers in Pandwani. The battle of Mahabharat is presented in such a way as if the locale of the battle which was fought somewhere in Gondwana.

The native place of the Pandwas is named as 'Jaitanagri' and the place of Korawas is named as 'Hasananagari'. Hasananagari is a corrupt form of Histinapur. Both Pandwas and Korwas have been described as cattle breeders who take their cattle to Kajaliwan for grazing. The expanse of Kajaliwan is up to the sea coast. They have eighteen lac cows, nine lac goats and innumerable elephants which they take for grazing. Korawas always ill treat Pandwas and while playing they always indulge in some mischief specially with Arjuna. Arjuna is thus harassed by Korawa brothers which Bhima does not like. He then takes the responsibility of cattle grazing so that he can teach them a lesson. From this point the development of Bhimas character starts in Pandwani narrative.

Hidimba who was an aboriginal girl in named is Satjogana, daughter of Vasukinaga in Pandwani. Kourawas were defeated in a game of 'Danda Dahori' by Bhima and then they conspired to kill him through a water game called 'Panidubki'. They gave him poisoned food to eat before the play and then drowned him in the sea. Bhima reached to 'Patalloka' (Under world) where he met Satjogana the daughter of saint Vasuki. Satjogana brought nectar from her father's nectar pool. She put some nectar in Bhima's mouth and he becomes alive. She prays goddess to get her married with Bhima and they were married in the Patalloka there itself. Now after spending some months with Satjogana Bhima was anxious to go to his brothers and mother. Satjogana took her to the sea shore. Bhima becomes vary pleased to meet them.

He tells them how he was conspired and poisoned by Korwas and drowned in the sea.

Korwas again conspired to kill all the Pandawa brothers. They constructed a place from lacquer called 'Lakha Mahal' and invited them to play dice and put the place to fire but Bhima hit hard his club on the ground and made a deep hole through which all the brothers escaped and went to Vairata city(Virat Nagar) to earn their livelihood. In the mean time in a Swayamber Arjuna was married to Dropadi. The name of the king of Vairata is Sangram Singh in Pandwani. Here Bhima kills Kichaka. To describe all these things here is to show how the epic Mahabharata is transformed in the folk tradition by incorporating the tribal elements.

The character of Dropadi has been described as a common Gond woman. The cultural and anthropological study of the Pardhan Gond epic Pandwani reveals some very significant features of the Gond society of Central India. Dropadi thinks that the five brother Pandwas have no proper means to fight the mighty Korwas who have a large army equipped with powerful arms. They have great commanders on their side, so why not kill the Pandwas by giving them poison and adopt Korawas. All the Pandwas died after eating poisonous food. Dropadi left the dead Pandwas in that condition and mixed turmeric with water in a pot and took it to Hastinapur. She poured that turmeric water on twenty-one Korawa brothers and became their wife.

When Kunti saw her sons dead, she went to Ayodhya to meet his brother Ramchandra and narrated the whole story. Then Ramchandra sprayed amrit (nectar) on the dead bodies of the Pandwas and made them alive. He also provided them staff of bel wood (aegle mamelos) to smell so that they become strong. After that Bhima started for Hansanapur to bring Dropadi back. When Karawas saw Bhima in fierce condition they got frightened. Dropadi consoled them not to be afraid and she would tackle him. Dropadi transformed herself in to a divinity and alighted her Khappar (plate) which resulted in to great fire all around. The nine kosa (eighteen miles) long tongue of Dropadi came out of her mouth and she went to kill Bhima holding khappar in one hand and a sword in another hand. There are several magical incidents in the narrative ahead of this episode in the battle between Dropadi and Bhima. Both try magic on each other. Dropadi under the influence of magic tries to eat all the Pandwa brothers. Bhima cut his little finger and offered to Dropadi by putting it in her Khappar. Dropadi is thus pacified and then she changed her attitude. Now she declares that she will eat the Korwas. Pandwani is full of magic, mythology, religion and rituals of Gond society. This is the Gond version of Mahabharata.

Gonds inhabit in large parts of Central India and their concentration is mainly located in Mahakosal and Chhattisgarh. The original place of Dewar community is also Mandla district. A large group of Dewars migrated to Ratanpur the Kalchuri kingdom. Both Pardhan and Dewar communities are responsible for propagating Pandwani in Chhattisgarh. Dewars also sing a ballad of Kalyansai Binjhia who was a diwan in the Kalchuri kingdom of Ratanpur with whom they trace their relationship.

The present mono theatre form of Pandwani is not a development of Pardhan and Dewar Pandwani. In reality it is a form based on the Mahabharat which has been developed by the non Brahmana lower castes who were traditionally giving discourse and performing Sankirtan. The Krishana devotees from Andhra used to travel to Mathura Vrandaban on pilgrimage through Chhattisgarh. In their contact the local performers developed a new theatre form which was influenced by 'Burrakatha' of Andhra. Mahabharata is also presented in Burrakatha. The Burrakatha performs use tambura and with the help of it they create mimes of different characters of Mahabharata. The narrative is both in prose and verse. Tambura is used continuously by the performers and that is why it was called Tambura Katha. In due course the letter 'T' disappeared and it became 'Burrakatha'.

In the theatre form of Pandwani the performers use Tamburas and with it's help create mimes of different characters of Mahabharata according to the narrative. In the initial stage the performers used to sit on a wooden seat in "Virasan pose" as they used to deliver discourse. The seat on which these performers sit is called 'Vyasgaddi' which establishes that they were 'Kathavachakas'. Later on some performers started miming and adding theatrical acting and perform moving on the stage. This is how the present form of Pandwani gradually evolved.

There are two styles of Pandwani one is known as Kapalika and the other is known as Vedmati. Kapalika means the style which is in 'smriti' or in oral tradition and Vedmati means which has a written text. The written word is known as Veda in Indian folk tradition. Although some performers claim that their tradition is Kapalika but which they all perform is more or less the text of Mahabharata for which they take help of Sabal Singh Chouhan's Mahabharata which is in verse form in Khadiboli (Hindi). The Kapalika Pandwani which is in oral tradition is Pardhan or Dewar Pandwani which still remains in balled form. As a matter of fact the theatrical form of Pandwani is Vedmati and not Kapalika.

The theatrical form of Pandwani which is Vedmati is not older than the beginning of twentieth century. Jhaduram Dwangan who is one of the famous Pandwani performer claims that he is the pioneer of this form, which is not fully correct. He himself has learnt this from his father. There were several other Pandwani performers prior to him. Jhaduram Devangan's contribution to the art is also very significant. His body language is also sharp and subtle. His contribution to Pandwani ha enriched the art immensely. He is the best artist to perform 'Shanti Parva' and 'Swargarohana episodes'. There are a number of other performers of great skill amongst Jhaduram's pupil. Punaram Nishad is famous for his physical gestures. Punaram, Chetan, Revaram Ganjeer have also enriched the form by their own style.

Some female performers have also contributed immensely to this art form. Laxmibai has developed a devotional style of her own. She also perform while sitting in virasan pose like Jhaduram and Punram, where as most of the other female artists perform in standing position. This provides them a very large space on the stage which make their performance more impressive. Teejanbai has done a lot of experiments in her performance. She comes from Behalia community and is most uninhibited in her performance. Through her robust mimes she thrills the audience. Shantibai Chelic is fine singer and by her singing she also has enriched Pandwani greatly. In recent years several male and female Pandwani artists have appeared on the scene.

Pandwani Performance

Pandwani is performed on a wooden platform, on a raised platform of a house, in an open veranda, in a courtyard of house or on the square of a village. The troupe is composed of five to six members of accompanying musicians, one main performer and one 'ragi' who supports the performer. The musical instruments which are used are Dholak, Harmonium, Cymbals and Tabla. Now a days Benzo and Casio are also becoming popular. The musicians sit on the wooden plank or platform in the back behind the performer.

Pandwani performer always holds a tambura in his or her hand. The association of tambura with the Pandwani performers have become a permanent fixer. Some performers even do not play on tambura and they only pretend doing so. They skillfully use tambura in miming the different characters of Mahabharata. While enacting the scene of Bhima the artist puts the tambura on his or her shoulder as a club, Arjuna by pulling the strings like an arrow, Krishana and Karna's characters by holding the tambura as reins of the horses yoked in a chariot. Tambura is suitable object for enacting different characters. Although the Pandwani performers follow the text of Sabal Singh Chouhan's Mahabharata but only a few use his verse as narrative. Every one improvises on the text according to his or her wit and skill. Chhattisgarhi artists have great sense of humour. "Rame Rame Bhaiya" like prop they use with prose and improvise it like verse. Everyone of them have developed such props of their own and the 'ragi' respects and also speaks 'hun' 'han' in between the pause. Those performers who perform in standing position moving on the dais have adopted some element of Nautcha theatre form. This is how they have made Pandwani more interesting and dynamic. Such experiments have given new dimensions to Pandwani and enriched the form further.

The assimilation of Nautcha elements in Pandwani like dance in between every pause breaks the monotony. Dance, drama, songs, mimes and music all combined have made Pandwani an impressive theatrical form. Although Pandwani in its theatrical form is not very old, but at the same time it has not become stereotyped and has a great potential to further grow. Such possibilities always remain there in folk theatre forms. In future the talented folk performers will enrich it more.

Presently there are several Pandwani artists on the scene. Jhaduram Dewangan who was the senior most artist died in the year 2002. Some of the outstanding artists are Punaram Nishad, Teajanbai, Rewaram Ganjer, Shantibai Chelak, Ritu Verma, Khublal Yadav, Laxmibai, Ramadhar Sinha, Laxmi Sahu, Prabha Yadav, Phoolsingh Sahu, Some Shastre, Puniabai, Chetan. All of them have created their identity. Most of them have given their performances throughout India. Some of them have also performed abroad through festival of India and other cultural exchange programs. Many new artists are appearing in this field and that shows that the future of Pandwani is bright.

17 CHAPTER

Rahasa

(A Traditional Theater Form of Chhattisgarha)

Rahasa is a traditional theater form from Chhattisgarha region. This form is popular in the Bilaspur district particularly and also in adjoining area of Raipur and Durg districts such as Simga and Bhatapara in Raipur District and Bemetara and Nawagarh in the Durg district. There is one more simlified form of Rahasa which is popular only in Dhamtari district. The word Rahas is derived from the word Rasa due to the difference in pronunciation in Hindi and Chhattisgarhi languages. The Rahas is the Chhattisgarhi version and form of Rasa Lila. The content of both the theater form is more or less the same, but the difference lies in the theatrical presentation of both the forms.

The Rasa Lila was evolved in the medieval India in Brandaban city of Braj region. the Rasa Lila theatre has incorporated the folk element of that region and the language also remains the Braj Bhasha whereas the Rahasa is a Chhattisgarhi adaptation of the Braj Rasa Lila in which a lot of folk element of Chhattisgarh has been incorporated. Though the language of Rahas is an admixture of Braj Bhasha and Chhattisgarhi both, but the theatrical styles of both the forms are quite different. The rich folk element of Chhattisgarhi culture has enriched this form which has given it a separate identity.

The Rasa Lila has been mentioned as Rahasa by some other eminent authors and performers also, such as Wajid Ali Shah the

Nawab of Awadh and Naval Singh of Braj region who has written a book, Rahasa Lavani on the same theme. In Awadhi.also the Rasa Lila is pronounced as Rahas Lila. Chhattisgarhi also belongs to the same linguistic family the eastern Hindi and hence the similarity is quite logical.

The history of Rahas Lila in Chhattisgarh is very interesting. This traditional theater has developed gradually in this area. Rani Durgawati of Gadha Mandla was a devotee of Lord Krishna. Two eminent poets of Ashtachhap were connected with her court were Chaturbhujdas and Kumbhandas . But some critics have disputed this fact. Any way, this fact is more important that the Krishna bhakti cult was very much in existence in the Kingdom of Rani Durgawati.

The Kingdom of the Kalchuri rulers was in the neighborhood and its capital was located at Ratanpur. The influence of Rani Durgawati on the Kalchuri Kings of Ratanpur was imminent. Gopal Mishra poet and devotee of Lord Krishna was in the service of Ratanpur rulers. He was born in the year 1636 and wrote a book of verse, Bhakta Chintamani in the year 1702. This book of verse contains the childhood adventures of Bal Krishna. It is also believed that he had gone to Mathura and Vrindaban on pilgrimage with other saint poets.

Babu Rewa Ram Kayastha was another poet and a Krishna devotee of Ratanpur who had written about seventeen books of verse. Five of his books were in Sanskrit language and twelve books in brajbhasha. His most famous work is supposed to be the Geet Madhava Mahakavya in Sanskrit language and contains 695 slokas (stanzas). This book was also adopted in Brajbhasha by the author himself. With the title as 'Rahas Lila'. The language of this work was Brajbhasha but not as pure as of Mathura Brandaban region. Babu Rewa Ram was born in the year 1814 and died around 1890/ 1891. It is believed that he had also gone to Mathura and Brandaban on pilgrimage and from there brought some Rasa Lila, Ramayan and Dan Lila, hand written 'Pothis' which were known as 'gutkas' in this region. With the help of those 'gutkas' he had prepared his own 'gutka' on 'Rahas Lila', that is why the language of this 'gutka' remained the same, the 'Brajbhasha'. The contents are also similar.

The first mention of Rasa is found in the Shri Mada Bhagwata in the tenth skandha as a part of Krishna Lila. In the medieval period, Brandaban became the centre of 'Vaishnava Bhakti' and all the saints and poets were attracted to visit the birthplace of Krishana and the place of his childhood. : the Brajmand around the beginning of yhe sixteenth century. This was inspired by Jaideo's Geet Goind which has stimulated the faith in the Bhagwat Dharma amongst the Hindus. From every corner of the country the Vashanava saints and poets made their pilgrimage to Mathura. Brandaban and other places to the Braj Mandal. Shankar Deo a Vaishanava poet of Assam made his first trip accompanied by his seventeen fellow pilgrims in the year 1481 A.D. and stayed there for ten years. He made his second trip in the year 1550 A.D. with a large group of 120 saints. After this incident Shri Madhavendra Puri from Utkal visited in the end of fifteenth century. Shri Vallabhacharya from Andhra in the year 1520 A.D. and Shri Chaitanya Mahaprabhu sent his six main disciples in the next twenty five years to Braj region. Maha Prabhu Hitharivansha came to Brandaban in the year 1533. Shri Hariram Vyas of Orcha made his pilgrimage to Mathura and Brandaban in the year 1534 A.D. Swami Haridas from Gujrat visited Mathura and Brandaban in 1543 and Shri Narayan Bhatta went to Braj Mandal in the year 1545 A.D. This is not the complete list of those saints and vashanava poets who went on pilgrimage to Mathura and Vrandaban but a list of those prominent saints amongst them.

This get together of such eminent saint poets who were devoted to Krishna and 'Bhagwat Dharma' created such a religious and heavenly atmosphere in Braj Mandal that this amalgamation resulted into the creation of a dance and drama form known as Rasa Lila. As Brajbhasha was a sweet language and belonged to the land of Lord Krishna, it became the language of the Rasalila. More over, the Vaishnava saints were very well versed in his language. The Hallishak dance which existed in the traditional dances of Braj , which is performed in a circle became ideal form of dance and drama. These saints and those others who came on pilgrimage to Mathura and Brandaban were so much influenced by Raslila that they took this form to their respective places and introduced it there. This is how Rasa Lila spread all over the country, in the sixteenth Century.

Narayan Bhatta a Vaishanava poet who came to Braj Mandal from Andhra and settled in Unchagaon near Barsana. In his two works 'Brajotsava Chandrika' and 'Premmankur' he systematically planned the Lila episodes and gave them an order. He also incorporated the theatrical elements and folk dances in the Rasa Lila. Later on the 'Ashtachhap' poets had contributed allot in the development of Raslila by their Verse.

Though the Rasa Lila is originated from the tenth 'Skandha', of Shri Mad Bhagwat and systematically given a dance and drama form by Shri Narayan Bhatta, but the Chhattisgarhi form of Rahas is based on two other books in addition to Shri Mad Bhagwat of Bope Deo. These books are Braj Bilas and Radhakrishna Bihar, written by Vaishanava Baba Brajbasi Das. Rewaram babu had compiled his Rahas gutka on the basis of these three books and by using some Chhattisgarhi words. This Rahas Lila of babu Rewaram was never printed but the Rahas performers used to obtain the hand written copies of the manuscript. This was the practice of that period. The Rahas performer used to copy from these hand written gutkas and that is how these gutkas spread all over the region. Some people claim that they have the hand written manuscript of Rahas of babu Rewaram, but it is difficult to as certain and verify this fact. All these hand written copies have some variation with each other which is quite natural also, as while copying the performers must have made some additions and alterations. But one thing is definite that some Rahas manuscript of Rewaram existed at some time. In the present times all the performers claim that their script is based on babu Rewaram 'gutka'. Shri RadhaKrishna Bihar ofThakur Shivprasad Singh is a published book which is supposed to be based on Babu Rewaram's text.

Rahas is considered is ritualistic act and it has its rites and religious discipline which must be observed strictly. The villagers approach the Rasdhari for the performance in their village. Tentative dates are also suggested. After consulting the 'Panchang', he would decide the dates for the 'rahas' performance. He would avoid the 'Panchak' dates. Any panchak should not fall in between the Rahas dates. After the agreement on dates between the villagers and the rahasdhari, the villagers would offer Rs. fifty one or one hundred and one with a coconut fruit and a 'dhoti' as token amount of booking. This makes the rahasdhari bound to perform rahas in that particular village on the agreed dates. Generally, the rahas dates are decided minimum one month before the performance as to make necessary arrangements and preparations. The villagers return to their village and install a ceremonial post which is called 'thun' on some auspicious date. The thun is installed on the open ground where rahas performance would take place. The place is cleaned and washed with cow dung. Some local Brahmin performs the rites for the installation of the rahas post. The villagers assemble on that spot. One elder person, or malgujar of the village or the person who is sharing the main financial burden is entrusted on behalf of all the villagers to perform the worship and other rites. Five person dig a pit for the installation of the 'thun' and when the pit is ready, turmeric, aeronaut and a rupee coin are kept in that pit. After the narration of mantras, the rahas post is erected in that pit. The post then is applied the religious thread and vermilion powder. Coconuts are broken and their a water is poured on the post as an offering and then the coconut prasad is distributed amongst the villagers.

The villagers discuss about the details of the programme and distribute the work to different persons. They also discuss about the shape and size of the stage which is known as 'beda'. The beda is constructed around the 'thun' which remains as a centre post. This post is covered with mud and paddy straw and then about eight feet high pillar is constructed around the thun. The pillar is made of bricks and mud which is about two feet in length and two feet in width. After this construction, the thun is considered as the Kadamb tree where Bal Krishna performed rasa lila. An abode is also erected on the pillars to keep an earthen lamp which is lit continuously from the starting day of the rahas till the last day.

The stage is made as a raised platform about two feet high from ground level. The beda is normally made in square size of about 20x20 feet. A revolving beda is also made which is revolved around the thun with the help of the audience sitting around it. This type of beda is expensive and hence constructed very rarely. The beda is open from all the sides but it is made facing the east. The entrance of the artist is made from the southern side. The audience sit on all the sides encircling the stage . The artists entry is made from a narrow strip left amongst the audience. The revolving stage is round in shape. The stage is richly decorated with flowers, mango leaf and twigs and the coloured papers. The stage is also covered with the wooded beams, bamboos and paddy straw and mango twigs.

The most important feature of the rahas theatre lies in the construction of huge earthen sculptures. The minimum number of such sculptures is ten and the maximum number is one hundred and twenty six. Nine images are installed on the stage which are Lord Ganesh, Riddhi and Siddhi, Radha and Krishna, Hanuman, Garuda, Brahma, Shiva, Parikshita and Shuk Deva.

The presence of these life size images of deities create tremendous effect and create heavenly atmosphere. Rest of the images are erected at different places in the village such as on the entrance of the village, on the main squares and places of prominence, the varranda or the front courtyard and of the village malagajarh's house and the village tank. All these images are related to the different episodes of rahas and thus create a dramatic atmosphere. These sculptures create Braj Mandal where child Krishna lived in the childhood made his sports.

The rahas images are constructed by an artist of Chitera caste. He is helped by villagers in transporting the mud, water and by mulching. The villagers also provide paddy straw and jute fibber which are also mixed with the mud as binding agent. In the first stage, the carcass is made with wood, bamboo and the paddy straw. After the carcass is made thick clay mulched with straw and jute fibers are applied and human shapes are given to the skeletons. Again a thin layer of mud mixed with jute is applied to give the final shape of the image. After this process the image is left to dry up. When the image becomes fully dry then the final coating of this paste of highly plastic clay is done. When the image becomes fully dry they are painted with colours. These colours are prepared by the Chitera himself. The images are painted according to their characters described in Shri Mad Bhadwat. The eyes are left unpainted and they are painted on the opening day of the performance after the worship by rasadhari. This act is known as opening of eyes and by that it is deemed that all characters have become alive and have come to either participate or witness the rahas performance.

On the stage, the images of deities are installed in a definite order. The small images of Radha-Krishna, Ganpati and Riddhi-Siddhi in the centre. Other images which are of life size are kept in this order- in the north eastern corner, the idol of Brahma is installed in the south corner the idol of Lord Shiva is kept in the south western corner, Parikshit and in the north west corner Shukdeo image is installed. On the eastern gate, Hanuman and Garud images are installed. In some villages where the village folk can not afford to spend on construction of images, they hang the printed pictures of all these deities. As these pictures are only two dimensional, whereas the clay images are three dimensional, the total effect of the clay images are more lively where as the pictures only fulfill a ritualistic formality. Some rasdharis have made wooden images also of the deities for regular use for their performance to avoid the unnecessary expenditure incurred on the clay images.

Other clay images are constructed at different places in the villages and their number also depends on the amount of money collected for the performance. Some well to do villagers prefer to spend their own money for construction of one or two images as it is considered auspicious, as well as prestigious also. Such images are constructed on the platforms or varandas of their own houses. The images of Kansa and Bhima are made in very huge size. Lord Krishna addressing Arjun in the Kurukshetra is constructed just on the village entrance. Though the episode covered in the rahas do not have any mention of Bhima, Arjun and Mahabharat's Lord Krishna, but conventionally these images are also constructed to create the age and times of Mahabharata. Other images which are made depicts different lila episodes such as Krishna Janma, Putna Wadha 'Makhan Chori', Brandaban Gaman, Bakasur Wadha, Radha & Gopi Milan Lila, Kaliya Daman, Panghat Lila, Goverdhan Parvat Lila, Dan Lila, Rasa Lila, Maharas Lila, Radha Vilap, Hindola Lila, Krishna Mathura Gaman Lila, Kubari Lila, Dhanusha Bhang, Kubalia Wadh, Kansa Wadh and Ugrasen Rajgaddi Lila. There are other smaller episodes also knitted in this great theatre which includes thousands of characters and when the rahas is performed on full scale one hundred and twenty six sculptures in total are made which are erected at different important places in the village. The atmosphere thus created takes the audiences in the Mahabharta era. The spectators feel that they are moving in the streets of the towns of Brajmandal and all the important personalities of that age are present around them.

On the opening day of the rahasa performance the keyman of the village, who is supposed to be the organiser of the programme performance the worship with his wife. Such person may be the malgujar or the Sarpanch or the rich farmer or the rich sahukar of the village who bears the main financial burden, of the performance. Rahas begins on the scheduled date. That day should not fall on the 'panchak' date and the rahas must be completed in either of the fortnights according to the moon of the Hindu Calender. To perform rahas partly in one fortnight and continue in the other fortnight is considered unauspicious.

Rahas is traditional theatre in which only male actors participate. The roles of females characters are also done by the male actors who dressup as female characters and do the make up suited to the roles. The actors are trained in the theatre craft, acting, singing and dancing by rasadhari. The rasadhari is supposed to be the master of all auspects of the rahas. Rasadhari is the director, singer and prompter combined when he is on the stage. The costumes of the Kings and their ministers are similar to the other traditional theatre forms of India. 'Jama' a coat like upper cloth made of velvet or satin and embroidered with silver and silk threads is put on by the Kings and their ministers. Coloured dhotis are put on as lower cloth. The Kings and queens put on crowns on their heads. The crown of Lord Krishna is elegantly made and a bunch of peacock feathers are studded in it. The actors in the female characters wear silken saris and also silk and satin ghaghras(skirts) and odhanis(upper cloth). The costumes of Yeshoda and Radha are gorgeously decorated.

Some characters specially the deities and the demons use masks which are made of papier-mache. These masks are richly decorated and are made in Mathura. Most of the dress material of the rahas theatre form are manufactured at Mathura only and from there all the rahas troupes purchase such material.

In the make up white soap stone powder, turmeric powder, black carbon(soot), pink colour, green colour, Indian neel, sandal paste, snow, talcum powder and lipstick are used. The make up is done by the artistes themselves with the help of each other. The noble characters are painted in yellow, pink and blue colours whereas the villains in the black and green colour. Krishna's body and face are painted in blue colour whereas Radha's make up is done in either yellow or pink colours. Wigs, false beards and mustaches are also used suiting to the characters.

Rahas is performed at two levels one at the level of content in which the episodes of the different lilas of the Bal Krishna are presented in a regular sequence. In between the two episodes natch and gammath the humorous skits presented. The actors participating in the main rahas theme belong to the rahas troupe where as the gammatt party which is also know as Chhaila party is included on contract by the rasadhari. In the troupe of rasadhari there are in all five to nine members. They include one or two chikara(string instrument) players, one tabala player, two dancers in female costumes and one torchbearer. There used to be a character who was known as mukutdhari, a symbol of lord Krishna, but now this character has vanished form the scene. The rasadhari is also included in this group who may play on chikara, harmonium or manjira. The famous rasadhari of good old days Manjhla Maharaj used to play on his chikara whereas the present day famous rasadhari Dadoo Singh plays on his harmonium. Nanaka Pandit plays on his cymbals only.

Though Rahas is a religious and tradition bound theatre but in Chhattisgarh it has become a secular theatre. Even the Satnamis and other low caste Hindus participate and perform in the rahas. It has also become a very democratic and liberal cultural platform in the sense that the total villagers contribute according to their capacity and participate in the occasion without any caste considerations. In Bilaspur and Durg districts the number of rasadharis from the lower castes is more than the higher caste Hindus. Even in some areas this theatre form is identified as Satnami Rahas Lila. The chiterias who make the images are also a low caste of untouchables in the Hindu caste hierarchy. All the rasadharis are called pandits without any consideration of caste and they apply sandal paste on their foreheads. The members of the rahas party wear Kurta and dhoti and keep a silk 'dupatta' on the shoulders. This is the common attire of the rahasa troupes.

The Chhaila party is composed of about six to ten members. In an average size troupe. There are two to three Nachkars(dancers), two 'jokkads', one 'pari', one tabla player, one dholakia, one Harmonium player and one cymbal player. The nachakars dressup as females and so also the pari. The pari makes her entry from the audience with lota(a jug) on her head. The jokkads and the pari tie the bells on their feet. They converse with each other in question answer form. In this conversation, they make critical remarks and comments on different social problems in satirical and humorous way, that the audience enjoys every bit of it. The jokkads and the pari are very quick witted their exchanges and gestures make the audience laugh all the time. The jokkad and pari conversation is followed by the dance performance by the nachkars. This whole combination is so funny and humorous that the rural folk of Chhattisgarh counts this ensemble as the greatest source of entertainment. After each serious episode of the rahasa the performance of the Chhaila party breaks the monotony and prepare the mood of the spectators fresh for the next episode of the rahasalila.

The rasadhari and his musical accompanists narrate the different episodes in verse form written by different medieval poets such as Jaideva, Surdas, and other poets of 'Ashta Chhap' School. This is supported by acting by the other artists. The rasadhari and his musical accompanists perform in two different styles they are in standing and sitting positions. In the sitting style the musicians sit on the north east corner of the state. This is known as the rahasa of 'baitha saz'. In the standing style musicians alongwith the rasadhari while playing on their instruments are moving around the 'kadamb tree' They fasten their instruments with their backs with the help of cloth pieces. This is known as 'knade sazka rahasa' or the rahasa of the standing musical accompanists. The later form is more popular as due to being in continuous action it is more dramatic and lively.

The musical accompanists of the Chhaila party perform the music sitting in the north western corner of the stage. The pari makes her entry from the southern side from the audience.

Rahasdhari or pandit who may belong to any caste performs his duty as a religious man. Once he enters the beda, he will remain there till the end of the days performance. He does not take even tea or water till the end of the performance. The performance of rahasa starts at ten 'O clock in the night and continue upto the sunrise in the morning. The rasadhari recites a couplet or an stanza from the text, which is repeated by other accompanists. He also explains the meaning of the verse in prose with his own commentary. The rasadhari and his party get rest when the actors perform or the Chhaila party then present skits in between the intervals. The rahasa performance continues for the whole night and it is completed in nine to ten days time.

The total village is in an atmosphere of festivity. The villagers clean their houses and while wash them or paint with cowdung mixed with yellow and red colours. They hang festoons made of coloured tissue paper or mango leaves.

The relatives and the married daughters are invited at the occasion. Spectators from near by villages upto a distance of about twenty five kms. come to see Rahasa performance on cycles, bullock carts and tractor trolleys. They stay for the whole night and return in the morning, when the performance of the day is completed. Every day about five to fifteen thousand spectators assemble to witness the performance. On the day of maharas and Krishna's departure to Mathura the attendance is supposed to be the maximum, as these scenes are emotionally very moving.

The performance of rahasa starts with the entrance of rasadhari and his party. Then Ganpati is brought by one artists in his lap. The artist who is made Ganpati uses a mask of Lord Ganesh with a long trunk. This papiermache mask is painted in red colour with ornamentation on the head. He also wears a yellow dhoti(pitambari) and a silken duppatta on his shoulder. He is offered a seat on which a carpet is spread. The worship of Ganpati is performed and blessings are sought for undisturbed completion of the rahasa performance. Ganpati gives his blessings and then taken back in the end by same person, as if he is an idol. After Ganpati, Sarswati, the deity of knowledge is also brought in the same fashion and her worship is also performed. She also gives blessings for the successful performance without any trouble and hindrance. She is taken back like a statue to the green room. After this, Bal Krishna is brought in the lap by one of the members of the party and his arti is performed. In the atribute of swaroopas he is worshipped like an icon of the god and given the respect as god and not a human being or an actor. This is how the 'purva rang' of the rahasa is observed.

Krishna and the two nachakar in the female attire are most of the time on the stage and present different 'lila' episodes according to the verse text sung by the rasadhari and his party. The nachakars perform dances suiting to the occasion and also repeat the verse rendered by the rasadhari. The same dancers converge quickly into the female characters of the rahasa as desired in the episode like 'gopis' or 'Yashoda'. Rahas is theatre of fantasy because the spectator is confronted with two worlds at a time, a real world in which Krishna is bahaving like any other common naughty child doing all sorts of childlike mischiefs and a heavenly world where he kills the powerful big demons and villains with his godly powers. The audience is in a complex mental state where he is a spectator in the theatre being performed and where he is seeing his godly world before his eyes. When he sees the demons like Putna, Bakasur, or Kansa being killed by child Krishna he forgets that he is seeing a theatre and believes that his god has come to his rescue and he would kill all these demons and villains. This combination and confrontation of lokik and alokik world create such a continous fatacy in the minds of the spectators that they are completely engrossed and lost in the mystic world of rahasa.

Not all the episodes are performed on the stage. Some lila episodes are performed at some places in the village also. The gobardhan lila, the Kaliya mardan lila, Kansa badh and maharas lila are performed at the selected sites in the village. The Kansa wadha is generally preferred to be performed either in front of the house of the malgujar or else on the main square of the village. The Kalia mardan is performed in the village tank. The effigy of Kalia nag is rested on the wooden floating platform where Lord Krishna arrives on a richly decorated boat and captures the Nag and put a thread through its nose. All the spectators assemble on the bank of the tank on that day. Similarly, on the day of Kansa badh the spectators gather at the main square where the huge statue of the cruel king Kansa is erected. The fight between Kansa and Krishna is presented with a lot of theatrical element. Kansa first fights with a sword in one hand and a shield in the other. After that he tries to attack with a bow and arrow and then with his gada(club). Ultimately Krishna kills the king Kansa. The villagers celebrate this occasion with bursting crackers. The villagers embrace each other also for this victory of the virtues on the vices.

The Krishna Mathura gaman lila' in which he departs for Mathura from Gokul is emotionally very moving. When he leaves the stage and pretends as if leaving for Mathura all the spectators get up including female folk and children accompany him. He takes a round of the streets of the village where he is greeted by the villagers. All the spectators are either wearing garlands are having flowers in their hands. Those who cannot get flowers, keep the green leaves in their hands. They embrace departing Krishna with tears in their eyes and voice choaked with emotion.

The artistes of the rahas are invited for meals by the well to do villagers. All the artistes take their meals at one house hold by whom they are invited. Normally one person invites them on single day and then on the other day some other person invites. When the invitation is accepted the person who invites lift the statue of Lord Krishna respectfully in the end of the performance and takes it to his home. The rasadhari and his party accompanies him. For the whole day they are the guests of that family. In the evening after taking bath they get ready and come strait to the beda with the statue of Krishna. On the completion of the performance the rahas party is given five to ten thousand of rupees, plus many gifts as grain, clothes, cows, bulls, ghee etc. are given. In addition to this , the money donated in the arti is also given to them, which is also about three to five thousand rupees, now a days. Rahasa performance is now a days a costly affair and the weak earning economy of the rural Chhattisgarh cannot afford to sustain this traditional theatre. The performances are organized very rarely now a days. The gingling bells of the nachakar(dancers) and pari are sought by some villagers as a souvenir and for this they give them money and gifts. Though the rahasa a theatre in lila style has been brought and introduced by the pilgrims or the touring rasa lila parties from Mathura Brandaban, it has assimilated so much local folk element in it that it has become an independent and distinct form now. The present form does not seem very old and might have been developed gradually in fag end of nineteenth century or even the beginning of the twelth century. Around nineteen hundred and ten the malgujars and the dau sahukars, traders and moneylenders were inviting Rasalila and Ramlila parties from northern part of India. This was considered more of a religious act than of an act of entertainment. These two lila theatres have been the greatest source of ethical and moral education for a very long time through out India. In rasa lila the spectator seizes to be spectator but becomes a part of lila and is lost in it. The image of Bal Krishna and the content of 'Bhakti',Vaishanavasur and Bhagwatdharma nitted so well with the rasa lila theatre that the audience is carried away by these elements to a divine mental state. The ten days of rahas creates an atmosphere of festivity and mysticism in the village where it is performed and also in the surrounding area. People remember the rahasa performance for years as this creates a deep impression on the minds and souls of the spectators.

The clay sculptures are left at their place where they are made. Gradually they get decayed and merged in the soil. The villagers think that their land has become sacred and pious.

❑❑❑

Nautcha

Nyayik Das Manikpuri. Director of Satya Kabir Nautcha Party. He is himself a renowned actor, dirctor of his troupe and acts as Jokkad

Nautcha

Jhumukdas Manikpuri. He is the top most actor of Nautcha and acts as Jokkad with Nyayikdas. At the age of eighty plus his wit and humour is remarkable. His combination with Nyayikdas make a perfect team. In this picture he is seen with two Paries

Bison horn dance of Dandami Maria

Dandami Maria or Bison horn Maria dancers. This is originally a marriage dance of the Dandami Maria tribe. As this happens to be the only dance form of the tribe, it is performed on all the occassions. This is the most elegant dance that is why V. Elwin rated it the best tribal dance of all the tribal dances of India. The crown or headggear is made of bison horns and it is decorated with a crust made of feathers of kingdrongo

Dewar Pandwani

A Dewar performer is rendering Pandwani legend on his sarangi. They call their chikara as sarangi. Dewar is a nomadic performer community of Chhattisgarh. In their reportary they have a number of ballads which include Pandwani, Gondwani, Ramayani and Dasmat Odanin which went to Gujrat with them and there it is named 'Jasma Odan'.
Only half a dozen ballad singers are surviving. After them this tradition will vanish. It is urgently needed that all their naratives should be reorded and preserved as archives

Natmask from Puri

Papiermache mask used in Naat. This is made by Jagnnath Puri shilpi community. Previously all the Bhatra Naat costumes and other make-up material was brought from Puri, but now a days it is available in adjoining western Orisa towns

Bhatra Naat

A scene of Bhatra Naat. Entrance of the king with the Vidushaka. All the characters make their entry through the audience. A corridor is left for this purpose among the audience

Oraon dancers

Oraon ritual dance.

Oraon is a large tribe who live in Chhattisgarh, Jharkhand and Orissa. Their famous dances are Karma and Sarhul. Both these dances are group dances in which both boys and girls participate

Oraon dancers

A group of girls have come to akhara (dance venue) to participate in their traditional attire. The dances are elegant and are accompanied with drum music

Bharthari singer

Chhattisgarh has a tradition of Bharthri singing. Although the singers have adopted the legenad partially. When Raja Bharthari of Ujjaiyini became a yogi accepting Gorkhnath as his mentor (Guru) and went to his own palace for alms, the queen, the darbarias and all the subjects of the Raj started weeping Not only that but evben his elephant and horse were weeping. From here the legent starts. The legend is full of pathos. This legend is rendered by the Jogies of Gorakhpur, Alwar and Ujjain also. In Chhattisgarh all the singers are female and do not belong to any sect

Nautcha

This is a scene of nautcha performance in which a Jokkad and pari are dancing

Nautcha

Najaria.

Najaria is an interesing character of Nautcha. In the beginning of the play she makes her entry from the audience. The jokkad calls her. She responds in a typical gentle voice and walks towards the stage dancing. She keeps two small pots (Lotas) on her head. There lotas are made of brass or bronze and extremely polished. When she dance the upper lota also moves. If the najaria takes round clockwise then the lota moves anti clockwise and if she whirl anti clockwise the lota rounds clockwise. In between the humaourous dialogues between the jokkad and pari and the dance creates a great spectacle

Nautcha

Najaria character of nautcha theatre. The female character is known as Najaria. There are one or two najarias in each play

Pandwani

Pandwani artiste Tejanbai enacting an episode of Mahabharta epic. Presently she is the topmost Pandwani performer. She is awarded padmashree and Padma-bhushan and many other honours of National and State level

Dandami Maria dance

Dandami Maria dancers performing bison horn dance

Nautcha

Nautcha artist Jhumukdas with the pari

Bhatra Naat

In this picture the Bhatra nat artists are enacting the episode Kichak Vadh from Mahabharata

The Oraon boys and girls are performing Karma dance. In Karma the boys and girls both participate

Oraon dance

The girls of Oraon tribe are performing Sarhul dance

Dandami Maria dance

**The girls of Maria tribe performing marriage dance.
The boys participate as drumers with their bison horn headgear**

Ganda baja

The Ganda Nishan players. Ganda bands are the village music band which are engaged by the rural people on all the auspicious occasions

Dewar dhummers

A Dewar mandar (drum) player. Dewar is a community of nomad performers

Nautcha

Nautcha performer Nyayikdas with the pari and Najariya

Pooja dance of Kanwar Tribe, Bilaspur

Pando dancers

Pando dancers performing their traditional dance

Jhaduram Dewangan, Pandwani artist enacting Shanti Parva

Naat

Narad Muni in a scene of Naat Jungal Samrat Tarjan Vadh

Naat mask

A papiermache Naat mask made at Puri. The Puri masks are used by Naat performers of Orissa and Bhatras of Bastar

Oraon

Oraon dancers performing a festival dance

Oraon

In Karma dance the dancers are creating the motives of Karam tree

A Baiga Woman
with Her Tattoo Motifs

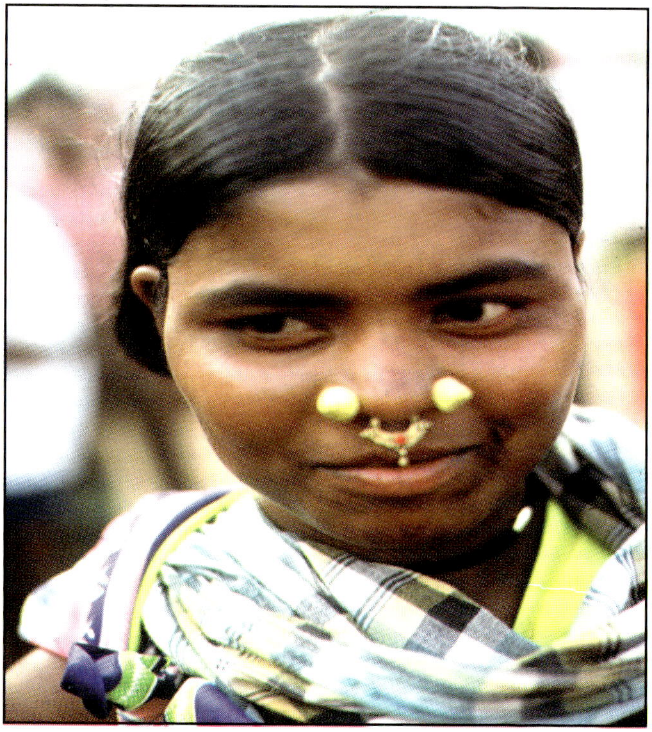

A
Bhatra
Dancer from
Bastar

Baiga Dancer in his dancing attire

Bharthari Singer rendering Bharthari Ballad

Bhatra Dancers

Bhatra Natya troop performing Kichak Vadh

Bhim and Kichak Fighting Gada Yudha (Mace Fight)

Binjhwar Karma of Bilaigarh

Bison Horn Dancers in a Madai (fair)

Dandami Maria Dancers in a Marriage Function

Dandami Maria Dancer with his Mandar (Drum)

Dandami Maria Dancers

Dandami Maria Women Attending A Marriage Function

Devar Natch of Mahasmund

Devar Natch of Rajnandgaon

Dewar Natch Party Nayapara Rajim

Dewar Dancer

Dropadi telling her woe to Bhim

Muria girls Ghotul in a Pata Dancing around Ghotul Pillar

Hulki Pata Muria Narayanpur

Jagar Singers of Bastar. Jagar songs are long Ballads in praise of goddess Laxmi and other deities

Kaksarh Dance of Muria Tribe of Bastar

Kamar Ballad Singer of Bindranavagarh

Mao Pata Dancers of Bastar, Garh Bangal

Muria Dancers of Narayanpur (Bastar)

Oraon Karma, Dancers from Jashpur (Surguja)

Oraon Karma, Jashpur

Oraon Musicians, Jashpur

Pando Tribe Sarguja performing Puja dance

Pandwani Performer

Panthi Dancers from Bhilai, Distt. Durg